Also by Larry B. Massie

Haven, Harbor & Heritage: The Holland, Michigan, Story   (1996)
On the Road to Michigan's Past   (1995)
Michigan Memories   (1994)
Birchbark Belles (1993)
Potawatomi Tears & Petticoat Pioneers (1992)
The Romance of Michigan's Past (1991)
Pig Boats & River Hogs   (1990)
Copper Trails & Iron Rails   (1989)
Voyages Into Michigan's Past   (1988)
Warm Friends & Wooden Shoes   (1988)
From Frontier Folk to Factory Smoke (1987)
    with Priscilla Massie
Walnut Pickles & Watermelon Cake: A Century of Michigan Cooking (1990)
    with Peter Schmitt
Battle Creek: The Place Behind the Products (1984)
Kalamazoo: The Place Behind the Products (1981) Expanded Edition (1998)

WHITE PINE WHISPERS

LIGHT HOUSE AND BARK HOUSES AT EAGLE HARBOR.

Charles Lanman sketched his childhood haunts on the River Raisin during the 1820s.

WHITE PINE WHISPERS

BY
LARRY B. MASSIE

The Priscilla Press
Allegan Forest, Michigan
1998

Please direct any questions or comments
concerning this publication to:
Priscilla D. Massie
2109 41st Street
Allegan Forest, MI. 49010
(616) 673-3633

Cover by Judi Miller Morris
Title Graphic by Devon Blackwood
Layout by Judy Barz
Proofreading Jacquelyn Taylor

ISBN: Soft Cover   1-886167-10-9
Hard Cover 1-886167-11-7

For the storytellers of yesterday and today who open our eyes
to the wonder of word pictures.

Four-year-old Maureen Massie delivered her first public
storytelling performance in August 1998 at the lighthouse at the
tip of the Leelanau Peninsula, much to the delight of the audience.

TABLE OF CONTENTS

Preface

Climb a tongue of highland lapping at the swamp. Sit upon a mossy cushion, green and specked with gold, and lean against the furrowed skin of a craggy ancient pine. Grant a ruddy sunset with fingerlings of clouds and a warm west wind heavy with the ripe fall forest scent.

Now listen to the white pine whisper of days forever gone. The great-boughed storytellers have centuries to say.

I have heard them paint Michigan as it was long before, two peninsulas' waiting bounty - blue water, red copper and towering green gold - when the only sounds that broke the primeval forest quiet were the panther's scream, the wolf pack's mournful howl, the gurgle of rivers and the faint pad of moccasined feet. Then came the French explorers, black-robed Jesuit priests and voyageurs in quest of gleaming beaver pelts.

The forest elders whisper how Chippewa canoes gave way to schooner captains braving billowing sweet water seas. The Ottawa lodges went too, when pioneers like ants hawed and geed their ox teams as they sought to tame the land.

I have felt them sigh of shanty boys whose thudding ax and rasping saw laid waste the wooded world - of the acrid smell of forest fires, lashed wild by hurricane winds to race from Lake Michigan sand dunes and hiss out at Huron's shore.

Sometimes they tell of copper miners pocking Keweenaw's rugged hills, of runaway slave women aboard the train to freedom and of generations of young men who left happy Michigan homes to march off to bloody battle, to Fredericksburg and Gettysburg, to Cuba and to France.

When the old pine needles rustle I have listened in wide-eyed wonder to tales of people, strange but true - of "bare torso kings" and fur trade queens; of presidential moral trials and priestly warriors brave; of the "sky pilot" who stormed Detroit and the white widow among the Chippewa; of the man who pulled the plug of Crystal Lake and the Teenie Weenie barrel house in lovely Grand Marais.

And now I pray these white pine whispers bring you pleasure, instill pride and inspire you to explore more of Michigan's majestic heritage.

Larry B. Massie
Allegan Forest, Michigan

Voyage to the Land
of the Stinkers

Jean Nicolet, the first European to explore the waters of Lake Michigan, and his seven Huron companions dipped their canoe paddles from dawn to dusk in early fall, 1634. Hugging the southern shore of the Upper Peninsula, they pushed cautiously toward their goal - a rendezvous with the mysterious tribe the French termed "Puans" - the Stinkers!

Periodically they beached their birch bark craft to hang gaudy presents on sticks in the sand so the tribesmen did not "mistake them for enemies to be massacred." Just the year before, Etienne Brule, the first French explorer to set foot on Michigan soil at Sault Ste. Marie in 1620, had been beaten to death, boiled and eaten by the Hurons. To have come so far only to be devoured by the Stinkers was a fate Nicolet did not relish.

Exactly a century before Nicolet's quest, Jacques Cartier had discovered the mouth of the St. Lawrence River. Under the command of French monarch Francis I he spent the succeeding eight years seeking a new and shorter water route to the fabled riches of the Orient. But when he faced the raging Lachine Rapids west of Montreal, and the gold and diamonds he found proved to be iron pyrite and quartz, he ended his search in bitter disappointment.

Cartier's failure and ensuing decades of civil and religious strife stymied the French from taking advantage of their initial North American discoveries. But at the dawn of the 17th-century King Henry IV again encouraged exploration and colonization of what became New France. The king granted a monopoly of the fur trade to Sieur de Monts. In 1608, de Monts' lieutenant, Samuel de Champlain, founded Quebec as a fur trading post. De Monts lost his monopoly two year's later, following the assassination of Henry IV, but Champlain continued as agent for the new monopoly, a coterie of French noblemen.

Over the succeeding decade, the man who became known as the "Father of New France" conducted numerous explorations. He reached the New York lake named in his honor and traveled up the Ottawa River thence to Georgian Bay, thereby establishing the famous fur trading route plied by generations of voyageurs and coureurs de bois.

During a foray to the south in 1609, Champlain and his Algonquin allies encountered a war party of Iroquois, traditional enemies of the Upper Great Lakes tribes. The Iroquois, who had never seen firearms, retreated in terror when Champlain blasted off his harquebus. That strategic blunder inspired an intense hatred for the French by the powerful Iroquois Confederation. The Iroquois enmity would restrict French exploration and development of the fur trade to the Upper Great Lakes and inflame a century and a half struggle for domination of the continent between rival European powers and their Indian allies.

As early as 1610, Champlain began sending select young men to the various tribes to learn their languages and cement friendships with the French. One such advisor and interpreter was the unfortunate Brule. In 1618, Nicolet journeyed from his native Cherbourg to New France. Champlain saw potential in the 20-year-old and immediately dispatched him to live among the Algonquin tribe on Allumette Island in the Ottawa River. Over the next two years Nicolet learned their language and customs. Despite periodic suffering and hardships - for weeks on end he ate nothing but the bark of trees - he came to prefer Indian ways over those of his civilized countrymen.

Returning to Quebec in 1620, Nicolet was sent to live and trade among the Nipissings, a Chippewa sub-tribe who dwelt along the northwestern Ontario lake named in their honor. During the eight years he remained with them, he further developed his wilderness skills and a fondness for the Indian life style. He became a "naturalized Nipissing."

Quebec fell to the English in 1629 and Champlain retreated to France. Nicolet remained, living among the Hurons. A treaty returned Quebec to the French three years later, and in 1633 Champlain again assumed command.

During his residence among the various tribes, Nicolet had heard stories about a mysterious people who spoke a strange tongue and dwelt in the unknown west. Legends told they had once lived upon the shores of a distant sea. Furthermore, they were said to trade with a race without hair or beards, resembling Tartars, and who came from the "Great Water," The Algonquins occasionally traded with this western tribe they called "ouinipeg," which loosely translated means "bad smelling water," the Indians' term for salt water. The French confused the meaning of the word and garbled it into "Men of the Stinking Water" or "La Nation des Puans" - the Nation of Stinkers. Despite that malodorous appellation, Champlain did not fail to grasp the significance of this intelligence - those hairless traders might well be Oriental and the "great water" a western sea leading to Asia. Could this be the long sought solution to the riddle of the water route to the Orient?

Too old to make the hazardous venture himself yet thirsty to unravel the mystery, Champlain decided to send his trusted interpreter and Indian expert Nicolet to seek out the Stinkers.

In company with the Jesuit priests Daniel, Davost and Brebeuf, Nicolet set out from Quebec in June, 1634. Amongst the supplies, trade goods and other gear stowed in the great canoe lay a carefully folded robe of China damask, gorgeously embroidered

Zoltan de Sepesky painted a stylized rendition of Jean Nicolet's
arrival in Michigan in 1634 for display at the Michigan Exhibit
during the 1933 Chicago Century of Progress Exposition.

with "flowers and birds of many colors," just the thing an ambassador to the people of the Orient would need to demonstrate his importance.

Paddling up the Ottawa River, Nicolet left the priests at Allumette Island and pushed on, portaging to Lake Nipissing and thence to the shore of Georgian Bay. To the west stretched as formidable a tract of terra incognita as Columbus faced in 1492. Convincing seven Huron braves to guide him to the land of the Stinkers, the party skirted the northern shore of Lake Huron.

Funneled into the St. Marys River, the explorer continued westward until the thundering Sault Rapids checked further progress. While at the future site of Sault Ste. Marie, Nicolet encountered a band of resident Chippewa the French called Saulteur (pronounced sewer, like the drain). After establishing rapport with the Saulters, who thrived by netting whitefish in the rapids, Nicolet paddled back down the St. Marys.

Days later he glided through the Straits of Mackinac to become the first European to view the broad expanse of Lake Michigan. Stifling his disappointment that it was a fresh water sea and not the salty ocean he sought, Nicolet pushed on, coasting the northern shore. At Big Bay De Noc he parleyed with the Noquets, a Chippewa sub-tribe.

Continuing southward, at the mouth of the Menominee he met the tribe of the same name, Algonquin for wild rice, which grew in abundance there and upon which the Menominees largely subsisted. While visiting the tribe, Nicolet sent ahead one of his Huron guides to alert the Stinkers that a French ambassador would soon arrive on a mission of peace. Nevertheless, during the following two days, as Nicolet and the six remaining guides paddled to the head of Green Bay, they took the precaution to stop frequently and hang presents on sticks along the shore.

As he neared his destination, Nicolet discerned a crowd gathered on the shore. Hurriedly slipping on his silk robe, he stepped ashore, firing a pair of flintlock horse pistols into the air. Women and children ran screaming in terror at the sight of "a man who carried thunder in both hands." But the braves greeted Nicolet reverently, carrying ashore the baggage of the "Manitouiriniou," or Godlike man.

The explorer had indeed reached the Nation of the Stinkers and to his chagrin found them not Mandarin traders but Winnebago Indians, their strange language a Siouan dialect he did not understand. Concealing his disappointment, Nicolet joined in the big celebration staged to honor his arrival. Four or five thousand members of various tribes gathered and the chiefs held great feasts. One chief regaled his guests by roasting 120 beavers, considered a great delicacy.

Following the festivities, Nicolet explored the surrounding country, voyaging up the Fox River and to the south, parleying with the Mascoutens, the Potawatomi and possibly the Illinois tribesmen. He also learned the true identify of the beardless traders who traveled the "Great Water." They were members of the Sioux nation, who shaved their heads leaving only a tuft of hair.

After wintering with the Winnebagoes, Nicolet set out on his return voyage in the spring of 1635, retracing his route to Quebec. Despite his failure to reach the Orient, Nicolet's grand geographic and ethnographic discoveries and his diplomatic success in furthering French influence among the new tribes pleased Champlain.

The "Father of New France" died a few months after Nicolet's return. But the futile search for a water passage across the continent, whose immensity the French had no concept of, would continue for another century.

It was a different mission, however - the saving of Indian souls - that brought the next Frenchmen to Michigan soil. In 1641, Jesuit Fathers Isaac Jogues and Charles Raymbault held the first Christian services in Michigan at Sault Ste. Marie.

In the meantime, Nicolet had married Champlain's godchild and been assigned as an interpreter at Trois Rivieres. In 1642, the intrepid explorer who had first braved the unknown waters of Lake Michigan drowned when his boat capsized in the icy St. Lawrence River.

Nicolet enjoys geographic immortality as a Minnesota county and a Quebec county and city. Counties in Wisconsin, Illinois and Iowa perpetuate the Winnebago tribal name. What is more, the first map of North America to show the Great Lakes in their proper relationship, drawn in 1650, designates what became Lake Michigan as "Lac des Puans" - Lake of the Stinkers. "What's in a name? That which we call a rose by any other name would smell as sweet."

Lacrosse: Michigan's First Team Sport

Life in modern Detroit bears little resemblance to that at the tiny French fort planted by Antoine de la Mothe Cadillac nearly three centuries ago. Yet surprisingly, some things have changed but little. For example, on any given glorious Michigan midsummer day in 1718 most women of Detroit area households might have been observed busily intent on the domestic drudgery that fell to their lot. But for the men, young and old, the focus of their attention was sports, the ball game in particular. Centuries before baseball, basketball and football successively ruled the season's entertainment, the original American sport - lacrosse - claimed a similar following among Michigan's native peoples.

Monsieur de Sabrevois, commandant of Fort Pontchartrain, penned a description of the region in 1718. Referring to the Potawatomi village located near the fort he wrote:

> *In summer they Play a great deal at la crosse, twenty or more on each side. Their bat [crosse] is a sort of small racket, and the ball with which they Play Is of very Heavy wood, a little larger than the balls we use in Tennis. When they Play, they Are entirely naked; they have only a breech-clout, and Shoes of deer-skin. Their bodies are painted all over with all Kinds of colors. There are some who paint their bodies with white clay, applying it to resemble silver lace sewed on all the seams of a coat; and, at a distance, one would take it for silver lace.*
>
> *They play for large Sums, and often The prize Amounts to more than 800 Livres. They set up two goals and begin Their game midway between; one party drives The ball one way, and the other in the*

opposite direction, and those who can drive It to the goal are the winners. All this is very diverting and interesting to behold. Often one Village Plays against another, the poux (Potawatomi) against the outaouacs (Ottawa) or the hurons, for very considerable prizes. The French frequently take part in these games.

The game described by Sabrevois and called baggattaway by the Chippewa was named lacrosse by early French observers. It is commonly assumed that the name stems from the French term *crosse* for the shepherd's crook-like crosier carried by bishops as a symbol of office. Pierre Francois Xavier de Charlevoix noted the resemblance between the crosier and the shape of the racket stick in 1719. However, the term *crosse*, which also translates as bat, had been applied to the Indian playing stick by the Jesuit fathers nearly a century before.

In any event, aboriginal tribes across the North American continent avidly played the sport as a form of recreation and as training in the art of war. Rules of the game differed from tribe to tribe. In some contests each player carried a single stick about three feet long; in others participants wielded a stick in each hand. Tribal customs determined the exact size and shape of the racket. The balls varied from wooden cores wrapped with rawhide to leather bags stuffed with deer hair. Some tribesmen, such as the Miami, drilled holes in theirs to produce a whistling sound when thrown.

Distances between goals ranged from a few hundred yards to several miles. Teams might number a dozen or entire villages of several hundred braves. Matches varied from a half hour in length to several days as the combatants attempted to hurl the ball against the goal, a pole or a natural object such as a rock, or between two uprights. The women and small children cheered the play. Lacrosse was solely a man's

Henry Rowe Schoolcraft included this steel engraving of a lacrosse game on the prairie in his monumental six-volume *History of the Indian Tribes.*

game, but less violent versions known as shinny and double-ball were played by women. The tribal shamen usually served as game officials. Rules were few, the play itself rough and injuries frequent.

Numerous French explorers, priests and fur traders who first described the land that would become Michigan recorded eye witness accounts of the game as played by the Potawatomi, Ottawa, Chippewa, Menominee, Miami, Mascouten, Sauk, Fox and Huron athletes who dwelt in the peninsulas during the first century of European contact.

Probably the first such description was penned by Father Jean de Brebeuf in the *Jesuit Relation* of 1636. At his mission to the Huron, located approximately 200 miles northeast of Detroit near the south shore of Georgian Bay, he found the reputed therapeutic effects of the game little to his liking:

There is a poor sick man, fevered of body and almost dying, and a miserable sorcerer will order for him, as a cooling remedy, a game of crosse. Or the sick man himself, sometimes, will have dreamed that he must die unless the whole country shall play crosse for his health; and no matter how little may be his credit, you will see them in a beautiful field, village contending against village as to who will play crosse the better, and betting against one another beaver robes and porcelain collars, so as to excite greater interest. Sometimes, also, one of these jugglers will say that the whole country is sick, and he asks a game of crosse to heal it; no more needs to be said, it is published immediately everywhere; and all the captains of each village give orders that all the young men do their duty in this respect, otherwise some great misfortune would befall the whole country.

While such epic matches may have preserved

the health of the country according to Huron belief, the sport often proved unhealthy for individual participants. Nicholas Perrot, whose memoirs preserved his many experiences as an explorer, fur trader and government official among the northern lake tribes from 1665-1701, described the rough play among the Huron:

> *At the appointed time they gather in a crowd in the center of the field, and one of the two captains, having the ball in his hand, tosses it up in the air, each player trying to send it in the proper direction. If the ball falls to the ground, they try to pull it toward themselves with their bats, and should it fall outside the crowd of players the most active of them win distinction by following closely after it. They make a great noise striking one against another when they try to parry strokes in order to drive the ball in the proper direction. If a player keeps the ball between his feet and is unwilling to let it go, he must guard against the blows his adversaries continually aim at his feet; if he happens to be wounded, it his own fault. Legs and arms are sometimes broken, and it has happened that a player has been killed. It is quite common to see someone crippled for the rest of his life who would not have had this misfortune but for his own obstinacy. When these accidents happen the unlucky victim quickly withdraws from the game, if he is in a condition to do so, but if his injury will not permit this, his relatives carry him home, and the game goes on till it is finished, as if nothing had occurred.*

Baron Louis Lahontan echoed Perrot's observations on the dangerous aspect of lacrosse in his *New Voyages to North America* (London, 1703): "... this game is so violent that they tear their skins and break their legs very often in striving to raise the ball."

Michigan Indian agent and ethnologist Henry Rowe Schoolcraft quoted a witness who had seen a player nearly killed during a match: "He stood in front of the player that was going to throw the ball, who threw with great force and aimed too low. The ball struck the other in the side, and knocked him senseless for some time."

When such accidents occurred the injured nurtured little ill will. Indian interpreter John Long, who described the Chippewa version of lacrosse in 1791, noted: "The Indians play with great good humor, and even when one of them happens, in the heat of the game, to strike another with his stick, it is not resented." Of course, in at least one famous episode the dangers of lacrosse were not restricted to participants. Alexander Henry's oft quoted eye witness account of the massacre at Fort Michilimackinac in June 1763, in which the spectators of that lacrosse game fared most unfortunate, springs to mind.

Far more typical of the lacrosse games enjoyed by the northern tribes is the account of a Sault Ste. Marie area Chippewa event penned in 1804 by Peter Grant, a fur trader who began his career with the North West Company in 1784:

> *Everything being prepared, a level plain about half a mile long is chosen, with proper barriers or goals at each end. Having previously formed into two equal parties, they assemble in the very middle of the field, and the game begins by throwing up the ball perpendicularly in the air, when, instantly, both parties form a singular group of naked men, painted in different colors and in the most comical attitudes imaginable, gaping with their hurdles [rackets] elevated in the air to catch the ball. Such a scene would make a scene worthy of a Hogarth or a Poussin.*
>
> *Whoever is so fortunate as to catch the ball in*

his hurdle, runs with it towards the barrier with all his might, supported by his party while his opponents pursue him and endeavor to strike it out.

He who succeeds in doing so, runs in the same manner towards the opposite barrier and is, of course, pursued in his turn. If in danger of being overtaken, he may throw it with his hurdle towards any of his associates who may happen to be nearer the barrier than himself. They have a particular knack of throwing it to a great distance in this manner, so that the best runners have not always the advantage, and, by a peculiar way of working their hands and arms while running, the ball never drops out of their hurdle.

If the ball did drop to the ground, the various tribes observed differing rules. Among the Huron, as we have seen, a wild melee resulted as everyone attempted to whack the ball or each other's limbs. But among the Miami, as recorded by Charlevoix after a visit to a village on the St. Joseph River, near the present site of Niles, in 1721, different procedures prevailed. If a player touched the ball with his hand or dropped it to the ground "the game is lost, unless he who has committed the mistake repairs it by driving the ball with one stroke to the bound, which is often impossible."

Indian players who accomplished great feats of play gained a celebrity status not unlike modern day sports heroes. Johann G. Kohl, a German tourist who traversed Lake Superior in 1854, observed: "Great ball players, who can send the ball so high it is out of sight, attain the same renown among the Indians as celebrated runners, hunters or warriors." While at the Apostle Islands, Kohl asked the local Chippewa to stage a game. But "though the chiefs were ready enough, and all were cutting their raquets and balls in the bushes,

Artist George Catlin painted this depiction of a western lacrosse player.

the chief American authorities forbade this innocent amusement." Bureaucratic spoilsports aside, by the era of Kohl's visit a number of white men had begun playing lacrosse themselves.

Ironically, Dr. W. George Beers, a Montreal physician, won title as the "father of lacrosse" because of his pioneering efforts to popularize the game among Canadians. He drew up rules and regulations in 1859. Over the decades as lacrosse became Canada's official national sport and clubs were organized in America, chiefly in eastern cities and colleges, the rules of the game as played by whites became more refined, the size of the field and number of players reduced, and a square goal replaced the original poles. Native Americans continued to enjoy their version of the game, often performing at state and county fairs and their own social gatherings.

In 1902, ethnologist William Jones observed a game of lacrosse played between two clans of the Fox tribe at Tama, Iowa. The match began with a declaration to the players by an elder: "We obtained this ball game from the Manitou. It was given to us long ago in the past. Our ancestors played it as the Manitou taught them. In the same way have we always played it, and in the same way all our people continue to play it." And then the old man offered some words of wisdom relevant to all who continue to enjoy the allure of any athletic endeavor: "Play hard, but play fair. Don't lose your heads and get angry."

Madam Laframboise:
Queen of the Fur Trade

The black-robed French who carried the cross to the Upper Peninsula wilderness had taught Joseph Laframboise well. The Mackinac Island-based fur trader followed the rituals of his religion with relentless fervor. Measured by his big silver key-wind watch, morning, noon and night he invariably knelt to mark the Angelus. True, he did sometimes ladle out whiskey to his Indian clients - to their harm, as he knew full well. But use of that watered-down, tobacco and pepper-spiked concoction was a deplorable necessity of his occupation and to have done otherwise would have proved a distinct business disadvantage.

Laframboise, his young wife Madeline, their baby son Joseph and two black slaves pushed off from Mackinac Island one early fall day in 1806 for the long voyage to their winter trading grounds on the Grand River. A dozen hardy voyageurs propelled two great bateaux piled high with trade goods. The merry French songs of the voyageurs rang out from dawn to dusk as they dipped their red-tipped paddles, hugging the shoreline except during the dangerous crossings of Little and Grand Traverse bays. A day away from their destination, the party camped near the mouth of the Muskegon River to trade and parley with local tribesmen.

A taste of fiery liquor always worked wonders in establishing rapport on such occasions. But when one ugly Ottawa brave, White Ox, demanded more, Laframboise refused him. Soon after, as Laframboise knelt in evening prayer in his tent, a musket shot rang out and the trader pitched forward, dead. White Ox had taken his revenge.

Though bereft of her soul mate, Madeline could ill afford prolonged grieving. The family's survival depended now on her strength. And she would rise to the occasion to blaze a remarkable career that would reverberate through the annals of early Michigan.

Madeline transported her husband's body to the Indian village at the mouth of the Grand River, the future site of Grand Haven, where she buried him. Born in 1780, the beautiful, graceful and spirited woman with "hair the sheen of a crow's wing" had grown up in this village following the death of her father, French trader Jean Baptiste Marcotte, when she was three months old. Madeline's mother, Marie Neskesh, was the daughter of powerful Ottawa Chief Returning Cloud. Marcotte's death prevented her from receiving the education in Montreal lavished on her siblings, but Madeline early displayed a flair for linguistics, speaking Ottawa, Chippewa, French and English fluently.

Her beauty and poise turned the head of Laframboise, scion of a famous Great Lakes fur trading family. He took her as his common-law wife when she was but 14, and in 1795 Madeline bore a daughter, Josette. The family spent each winter trading along the Grand River but maintained a permanent home on Mackinac Island. There in 1804, a priest solemnized their union in an official ceremony and duly recorded the event in the Mackinac Register.

Following Laframboise's murder, Madeline might well have continued to dwell among her relatives at the Grand Haven village or on Mackinac Island. Instead she chose a courageous course that few women of her time would have attempted. She determined to carry on the fur trade herself and proceeded to her post near present day Ada.

During the course of that first winter, a party of Ottawa captured White Ox and brought the murderer to Madeline to decide his fate, a quick death by shooting or slow torture by fire. Instead of demanding "an eye for an eye," as was the Ottawa custom, Madeline deliv-

This modern painting of Madame Laframboise hangs in her home on Mackinac Island, now the Harbour View Inn.

ered an eloquent speech, reminding the Indians of the pious nature of her husband and his many good deeds. Then she said, "I will do as I know he would do, could he now speak to you; I will forgive White Ox, and leave him to the Great Spirit. He will do what is right." The Ottawa released the murderer to suffer the shame of a pariah for the rest of his life.

Madeline returned in June to Mackinac Island, her bateaux laden with great gleaming bales of beaver pelts and her husband's disinterred body for reburial in the family plot. Three months later, having sold her furs at a tidy profit and restocked her supply of trade goods, including numerous casks of fire water, she again made the arduous journey to the Grand River. And so it went, year after year; plying the seasonal cycle of the fur trade she built upon her husband's reputation as a fair trader, notwithstanding the liquor dispensed, and amassed as much as $5,000 to $10,000 profits annually at a time when voyageurs earned less than $1.00 per day for their herculean labors.

Following the War of 1812, she faced increasing competitive pressure from John Jacob Astor's American Fur Company which established a near monopoly in the American fur trade. But through cunning, compromise and diplomacy Madeline adroitly fended off attempts to swallow up her operation

Madeline's continued success allowed her to give her children the Montreal education she had been denied. Daughter Josette grew into a sophisticated dark-eyed beauty, the belle of Mackinac Island. In 1817, a dashing young officer stationed at the fort, Capt. Benjamin Pierce, whose younger brother Franklin would be elected president 35 years later, married Josette. The wedding, staged in the largest dwelling on the island, was long remembered as the social event of the decade. Always proud of her Ottawa heritage, Madeline dressed in full Indian finery, including a gorgeous deerskin tunic embroidered with colored beads and porcupine quills, to mingle with gold braid-bedecked soldiers and satin-gowned ladies.

The newlyweds assumed their places among the cream of island society. Two children were born to the Pierces, Josette Harriet and Benjamin Langdon. In 1821, death took both Josette and her infant son, Benjamin.

Heartbroken, Madeline retired from the fur trade that year, selling her flourishing post to Rix Robinson of the American Fur Company. She moved to the great square house financed from fur earnings and erected by her son-in-law. Renovated, the structure survives as the opulent Harbour View Inn.

During the following quarter century Mackinac Island would be her domain. For one used to the peripatetic and exciting life of the fur trader idle retirement held little appeal. Madeline launched numerous projects. She taught herself to read and write both French and English. Surviving examples of her correspondence with friends document beautiful handwriting and fine grammar.

Having tasted the fruits of education, she did much to further its development on the island. She allowed the Presbyterian missionary, the Rev. William Ferry, to launch his boarding school for Indian children in her rambling home in 1823. Seven years later she assisted Father Samuel Mazzuchelli in creating a Catholic school on the island.

Mazzuchelli, the first resident priest on the island since 1765, lived in Madeline's house when he arrived in 1830. Her home also became a haven for other distinguished visitors to the north country including literary luminary and transcendentalist Margaret Fuller Ossoli and French traveler Alexis de Tocqueville. Through her own strong will the half-breed widowed squaw had risen to become the celebrated Madame Laframboise whose home served as a salon, an oasis of culture on the frontier. There, as fellow fur trader and Chicago pioneer Gurdon Hubbard remarked, he and friends could feel "fully at leisure" on Sunday afternoons.

Madeline also practiced philanthropy, providing for destitute, aged and orphan island Indians. In 1837, resident Indian agent Henry Schoolcraft described her taking care of "a poor decrepit Indian woman" who had been abandoned by her own relatives.

Madeline continued to devoutly practice her religion. As Joseph had taught her, "the moment the Angelus sounded, she would drop her work, make the sign of the cross, and with bowed head and crossed hands say the short prayer." And it was her beloved Catholic church that benefited most from her generosity. Her largesse helped make possible the ministrations of Mazzuchelli and subsequent priests. In the mid 1820s, she donated the lot adjacent to her house as a new site for St. Anne's Church. In 1846, when Madeline died, she was laid to rest beneath the floor of the church beside Joseph and Josette.

An early view of Madame Laframboise's home captures it as a mecca of culture on the frontier.

Charles Hoffman's Ride Across The Peninsula

On a miserable mid-December day in 1833, Charles Fenno Hoffman neared the forks of the Kalamazoo River, the future site of Albion. Blinded by driving snow that erased the trail and plastered over hatchet blazes on the trees, his mount slipping and floundering at every step, the one-legged writer from New York wandered lost in dense forest.

Suddenly he emerged from tangled growth onto a burr-oak opening. Despite his predicament, Hoffman marveled at the beauty of the pristine Michigan terrain. The park-like oak openings, where broad-boughed trees stood at regular intervals, appeared more like a cultivated pear orchard. Burned-over yearly by the Indians to enhance hunting, the level landscape lay devoid of underbrush or briars.

He saw great herds of deer bounding away and "the sight of those spirited-looking creatures sweeping in troops through interminable groves, where my eye could follow them for miles over the smooth snowy plain, actually warmed and invigorated me." Luckily, the half-frozen and weary rider discovered a series of blazed trees, the only guideposts in the peninsula, that led him back to the trail heading west, euphemistically termed the Territorial Road.

"What a country this is!" Hoffman rhapsodized, remembering his recent conversation with a settler. When asked about the quality of the soil, he had answered: "A pretty good gravelly loam of 18 inches; but I think soon of moving off to Kalamazoo, where they have it four feet deep, and so fat it will grease your fingers." Hoffman predicted "railroads and canals will make one broad garden of Michigan."

It was a happy day for Michigan history when, in early October 1833, Hoffman set out to become the first tourist to take "a winter view of scenes upon the

Indian frontier." Other literary luminaries of the period had traversed Michigan by stagecoach then written about it: - the testy British, Patrick Shirreff and Joseph Latrobe in 1833, and Harriet Martineau with her big ear trumpet three years later. But Hoffman was the first to brave an equestrian romp across the snowy peninsula. His travel narrative, *A Winter in the West,* published in 1835, offers the most spirited and colorful description of the territory and its nascent settlements during the watershed pre-statehood pioneer era.

Born in New York City in 1806, Hoffman at the age of eleven suffered an accident that so crushed his right leg it had to be amputated above the knee. To compensate, he trained rigorously as an athlete. Entering Columbia University in 1821, his studies took a back seat to sports and he flunked out three years later. He joined his father and half-brothers as a lawyer in 1827, but the bar cloyed in comparison to his true calling as a writer.

After three years he abandoned his practice to serve as co-editor of the New York *American* and later as editor of a new popular periodical, the *Knickerbocker Magazine.* Adventure beckoned in 1833 and Hoffman relinquished his office chair for the saddle.

Riding a circuitous route to Pittsburgh then by stage to Cleveland, he boarded the steamer *New York,* "crowded with boxes, bales and the effects of emigrants, who were screaming to each other in half as many languages as were spoken in Babel," for a smooth passage to Detroit. He found that ancient French village bustling and booming as the staging ground for the hordes of immigrants pouring into Michigan to take up government land at $1.25 an acre. Later, when Hoffman had met enough Michigan pioneers to judge, he decreed them "much superior in character to the ordinary settlers of a new country."

And the reason, he deduced, lay in the federal government policy that made land available in tracts of 40 acres or more payable in cash only. At a time when laborers earned 50 cents or less for a 10 to 12 hour workday, $50 was a sum saved only by the industrious and enterprising - in short, improvident nere'-do-wells need not apply for Michigan citizenship.

After forays to Dearborn, which had sprung up around a new federal arsenal, and Monroe, where he interviewed survivors of the River Raisin Massacre of 20 years before, Hoffman forwarded his trunk to Niles,

Charles Fenno Hoffman liked what he saw during his winter's ride across the territory in 1833.

packed saddlebags with extra shirts and leggings, slung on a shotgun, mounted his "stout roan" and cantered westward.

Traveling daily from dawn to dusk, Hoffman took lodging occasionally in village taverns but more often at lonely log cabins. True to the frontier creed, he encountered instant hospitality among pioneer families. At his first stop east of Tecumseh he barged in on a family at supper. They amiably waved the stranger to a chair. Helping himself to a big ladle of steaming cornmeal mush, he "fished up a cup from the bottom of a huge pan of milk and poured the snowy liquid over the boiled meal that rivaled it in whiteness." The corn, his host boasted, came from plants 16-feet-high. That same virgin soil grew wheat "as tall as a man's head." For good reason, except for some wives who lamented the lack of society, Hoffman found settlers at far-flung cabins almost universally delighted with their new holdings.

As the writer pushed west he savored many other succulent frontier meals: breakfasts of "hot rolls and tea, large slices of pork swimming in gravy and a dish of mealy potatoes," suppers of pared potatoes, spongy wheat bread, cranberry sauce, honey in the comb and venison steaks. Wild game, particularly grouse and deer abounded. At three separate cabins he saw children playing with pet fawns.

Near Spring Arbor in Jackson County, Hoffman encountered a traveling band of Ottawa with "fluttering blankets, gleaming weapons and gaudy equipments" who greeted him with "Boju" and passed on. Contrary to later developments culminating in the removal of the Potawatomi at bayonet point across the Mississippi in 1840, Hoffman noted that Michigan pioneers "generally appear to treat this ill-fated race with a depth of kindness and consideration that might well be imitated in other sections of our frontier." Near Jackson, he noticed next to a cabin an Indian burial plot that was frequently visited and weeded by the survivors. The settler had obligingly fenced it to keep out livestock.

Several days sloughing along mud-choked trails, through driving sleet and snow, and wandering lost for hours, brought Hoffman to Marshall, an oasis of comfort. He lodged at the two-year-old community's grand Marshall House. While the walls of the new hotel had yet to be plastered, he noticed "the bar-room wore already the insignia of a long established inn, with notices and broadsides tacked everywhere."

West of Marshall, the many lakes and other "scenic gems" he skirted drew praise worthy of a tourist bureau. He took "singular pleasure in surveying these beauties, as yet unmarred by the improving axe of the woodsman, and unprofaned by the cockney eyes of city tourists." Hoffman preferred the scenery of Michigan's lakes, meadows and forests to classic lands of the Mediterranean, eschewing a "moldering column for a hoary oak."

Hoffman spent the following night in the settlement entrepreneur Horace Comstock had named after himself. He observed a "flourishing establishment, a frame store and several log cabins, with two or three mills." Bypassing Bronson, which despite winning the coveted county seat designation over Comstock in 1831 would lag behind until relocation from White Pigeon of the federal land office in 1834, Hoffman spurred his steed toward Schoolcraft, then Kalamazoo's leading community.

After galloping across wind-swept Prairie Ronde, the half frozen horseman limped into the village tavern. The cheery barroom teemed with "a salad of society." Hoffman shared a round of hot toddies with a convivial "long-haired 'hoosier,' a couple of smart looking 'suckers' from the southern part of Illinois, a keen-eyed, leather belted 'badger' from the mines of Wisconsin, a 'red horse' from Kentucky, and a native 'wolverine,' dressed in a white chapeau, Indian moccasins and red sash."

Hoffman found life in the community clustered at the big island of woods in the center of the prairie untypical of the frontier. The rich soil and ease of cultivation, he speculated, afforded the residents ample leisure. Villagers enjoyed fox hunting on horseback with packs of hounds and the excitement of wolf, bear and badger baiting, that is, pitting packs of dogs against disabled wild animals. Schoolcraft prided itself on the "number of fine running horses, blooded dogs and keen sportsmen it has."

From the settlement of sportsmen, Hoffman rode south to White Pigeon, "a pretty village of four years' growth," then to "the flourishing town of Niles," where he boarded a wagon for Chicago. Bidding adieu to Michigan for the "land of the Hoosiers," he cast a parting favor: "To no scenery of our country that I have yet seen is the term Arcadian more applicable than to the rich and fairy landscape on the western side of the peninsula, watered by the Kalamazoo and the St. Joseph's."

Hoffman pursued his western itinerary, visiting Chicago, Galena, St. Louis, Louisville, Cincinnati and Lexington, Kentucky, before reaching his New York home in June 1834. He continued his literary career, editing a series of newspapers and magazines and publishing eight volumes of travels, novels, poetry and essays. Tragically, the bane of many a writer struck - an attack of mental illness. In 1850, authorities committed Hoffman to the State Hospital in Harrisburg, Pennsylvania. There, until his death 34 years later, the literary traveler who found so much to admire in frontier Michigan remained, "happy, amiable and sociable, but completely insane."

Snakes Alive!
The Birth Of Allegan

Kalamazoo-based land speculators Stephen Vickery and Anthony Cooley thought the peninsula formed by the big python-like writhes of the Kalamazoo River at the future site of Allegan just about one of the most alluring spots in southwest Michigan. With a fall of about eight feet in the river there, construction of a mill race promised excellent water power. The site lay near the center of the county and thereby stood a good chance of being designated county seat, an asset second only to hydraulic potential. And to the north stretched a seemingly boundless tract of virgin white pine - "green gold."

As Vickery and Cooley tramped the terrain in the summer of 1833, visualizing the town they could plat out and the mountains of money to be made by selling off little lots, only one problem nagged at their get-rich-quick schemes: the sibilant slither and warning rattle of massasaugas, the ugly-tempered little swamp rattlers that infested the site.

When the War of 1812 ended in 1815, rendering the Northwest frontier again safe for settlers, hordes of immigrants loaded families and possessions into ox-drawn covered wagons and rumbled west in search of a new life. They took up homesteads in Ohio, Indiana and Illinois but avoided Michigan Territory like the plague, in part due to rumors predicated on early reports by a Buckeye surveyor general which branded the lower peninsula a vast swamp, a slough that bred vicious beasts of prey, clouds of malarial mosquitoes and massasaugas.

Those few who braved the unknown terrain did indeed encounter more snakes than "you could shake a stick at." Benjamin O. Williams, who pioneered Oakland County in 1818, for example, recalled killing twelve rattlesnakes alone, while mowing marsh hay one morning. His brother Ephraim walked about 30 feet dragging a snake that had snagged its fangs into the bottom of his trousers before he discovered and shook it off.

An ugly tempered massasauga coils beside the little prickly pear cacti that are also native to Michigan.

Despite the serpents, in 1825 when the opening of the Erie Canal facilitated travel to Detroit, stories circulated in the east of the peninsula's lush prairies, park-like oak openings and endless tracts of big trees launched a land rush of epic proportions. Many who set out for "Michigania" hailed from western New York, sons and daughters of those who had pioneered the Genesee Valley a generation before. Most were bona fide settlers, eager to acquire their pick of the land at the standard government rate of $1.25 an acre and cast their lot with the Wolverine State. But many others were simply speculators, seeking to invest in large sections of choice land to be sold to later immigrants at a steep mark up. The cagiest of the speculators opted for town sites they might plat into lots and sell for hundreds or thousands of times their original cost.

Wealthy eastern capitalists formed syndicates to invest in cheap Michigan land and dispatched agents into the wilderness to select prime tracts. Other moneyed land-lookers preferred to journey to the frontier to stake out ideal locations. In an era when water power provided the dominant energy to operate machinery, any town seeking viable industry required plenty of flowing water.

During the 1830s, entrepreneurs soon dotted the length of the Kalamazoo River with frontier settlements: Albion, Marshall and Battle Creek in Calhoun County, rival communities Bronson and Comstock, each named after its promoter, and in Allegan County came Otsego, Pine Creek, New Richmond and Singapore at the river's mouth. The founders of each envisioned their town emerging as the new metropolis of the northwest.

Vickery and Cooley stifled their concerns over the rattle and hiss and rode to the federal land office in White Pigeon, where in late summer 1833 they purchased a portion of the land now comprising Allegan. Later that fall, George Ketchum of Marshall bought an adjacent parcel. In November 1833, Elisha Ely, a wealthy businessmen and veteran of the War of 1812 from Rochester, New York, traveled through the territory seeking a good investment. After viewing the site of Allegan, presumably when the snakes had holed up for the winter, he promptly bought a one-third interest in the property from Vickery and Cooley. Those Kalamazoo speculators, Ely and his son Alexander platted, the village of Allegan. The following June, the Elys sent in the Leander Prouty family from Rochester. The Proutys constructed two log cabins and grubbed the ground for a mill race. Then, for some unexplained reason - maybe the snakes - ownership of the site of Allegan got tossed around like a hot potato.

In October 1834, Ketchum's bother Sydney, land agent for a syndicate of Boston investors, bought out Vickery and Cooley's share. The new proprietors of Allegan were Samuel Hubbard, a Massachusetts Supreme Court Judge, Edmund Monroe, Pliney Cutler and Charles C. Trowbridge of Detroit. Despite the fact that Allegan Street names continue to honor their memory, those members of the Allegan Company remained absentee landlords. The only partners to reside in the settlement were the Elys. Elisha went on to represent Allegan County in the Territorial Legislature and later to serve as a regent of the University of Michigan.

Intent on making their endeavor a success, the Elys spent the winter of 1834-35 hacking out primitive roads and collecting provisions. In April 1835, they started construction of a dam and canal for a saw mill. Its giant jig-saw-like blade began ripping through timber the following fall, effectively ending the community's brief log cabin era.

In the meantime, the Allegan Company, sometimes called the Boston Company, had hired a jack-of-all-trades from Massachusetts named Oshea Wilder to survey the site and lay out lots. Wilder set about his task in May 1835, but because he had not quite mastered his craft or, maybe, because of the snakes, his miserable surveying job rendered village streets about as crooked as a serpent's tail.

While under the employ of the Allegan Company, Wilder was appointed by Territorial Governor Stephens T. Mason on a commission to designate the Allegan County seat, along with Kalamazoo attorney Cyrus Lovell and Isaac E. Crary from Marshall, who later served as the state's first representative to Congress. Needless to say, with Wilder's assistance Allegan handily won out over its closest rival, Otsego.

Following that fillip to its future, in June 1835, the Joseph Fisk family arrived from Rochester, where the Elys had busily promoted their paper city, to purchase the first village lots in Allegan. Soon, a rush of settlers, mostly from Rochester and western New York, joined them. As those pioneers worked at clearing off their lots and constructing dwellings they encountered numerous massasaugas contesting control of their native domain. Out of desperation, the settlers strapped swathes of bark to their legs and, thus armored, continued to wrest Allegan from the grip of the vipers.

In November, the first merchant opened shop. The following month the company began building a Presbyterian church. Completed in May 1836, the

**Pioneer physician Dr. Osman D. Goodrich
sketched a forlorn Allegan in 1840.**

structure fell victim a few days later to a conflagration that spread from a gigantic bonfire ignited by a workman hired to rid the site of the huge hardwood trees that thrived there.

Despite such temporary setbacks, the company town of Allegan prospered. In November 1836, Alexander Ely wrote Indian agent Henry Rowe Schoolcraft describing the town's growth. Schoolcraft, incidently, had cobbled together out of Ottawa and Chippewa words the names of numerous Michigan counties, including Allegan, an irrelevant though euphonious amalgam meaning "Lake of the Algonquins." Ely proudly described Allegan as having "three stores, two large taverns, a cupola furnace, a chairmaker's shop, a tailor's shop, a schoolhouse 20 by 40, costing $1,200; about 40 frame buildings, and over 500 people." The schoolhouse, originally located on the south side of Trowbridge Street,doubled as the county's first courthouse where itinerant circuit court judges presided.

By 1837, when Michigan entered the Union, Allegan's population numbered around 700. A physician and two lawyers had hung out their shingles. The village sported a post office as well as the Bank of Allegan which began printing and circulating "wildcat" paper money backed by little, if any, gold. Workmen were in the process of constructing two bridges across the Kalamazoo River to replace the cumbersome ferry service. The initial industry, sawing lumber, prospered with nearly four million board feet floated down the river to market the previous season.

The county seat's future looked rosy, indeed. But before 1837 had ended, a severe depression gripped the eastern states, precipitated, in part, by President Andrew Jackson's Specie Circular of 1836 which required government lands be paid for in hard money, not the nearly worthless wildcat currency churned out by institutions such as the Bank of Allegan. Initially, Michigan remained insulated from the worst effects of the depression, largely because of the new state's boundless optimism. But by 1839 the rush of new settlers into Michigan dwindled and commodity prices on the frontier came crashing down. Businesses went bankrupt, banks closed forever, and much of the prime land grabbed by speculators reverted to the public domain via back taxes.

Allegan fell on hard times. Everybody owed the Allegan Company and nobody had cash to pay. Company orders for goods and services circulated like currency. The proprietors continued to pump some money into the town for a few years, but by 1844 they, too, were in dire straits. That year, Alexander Ely and his brother Elisha D. pulled up stakes and headed farther west where they helped pioneer Cedar Rapids, Iowa. Five years later, all Allegan village property that had not been purchased was sold at public auction and the proceeds divided among the numerous creditors.

The little community lost a good share of its population, but enough settlers had the grit to stick it out until the economic picture brightened in the 1850s. New industries came to Allegan: the Born wagon factory, the Oliver Furniture Co. and a ship building operation that launched several vessels on the Kalamazoo.

Unlike fellow Kalamazoo River towns, such as Pine Creek near Otsego and Singapore buried beneath sand dunes at the mouth of the river, Allegan would remain a vital community. Now only the coils of the Kalamazoo and the city's serpentine streets remind that the city was once the lair of the massasauga.

Potatoes, Pork & Pone: Pioneer Cookery

Anson Van Buren had the "Michigan appetite," and he had it bad. When his family emigrated from western New York to Calhoun County in 1836, settlers had warned the 13-year-old about the ailment. And sure enough, within a few months a ravenous craving continually gnawed at his stomach. He was so hungry he could have "ate a biled Indian."

The Herculean tasks Michigan pioneers faced from dawn to dusk, chopping down forest giants, rolling the logs into huge heaps to be burned, hawing and geeing stubborn oxen around great stumps in an effort to plow the tough virgin soil, and all the while swatting hordes of insect vampires, took a tremendous caloric toll. But with victuals scarce, standard fare day in and day out consisted solely of bread, potatoes and pork - for those lucky enough to have even those staples. Not enough fat hung on the average pioneer to grease a skillet. Even frontier pettifoggers and politicians waned thin as a rail.

Van Buren remembered: "It seemed that all we labored for was to get enough to eat. Fruitless toil, for we were hungry all the time." A half century later, when he had become a successful insurance agent in Galesburg, an episode from those early lean years remained vivid.

Left home alone one Sunday morning while the rest of the family went to hear an itinerant preacher hold forth in the local schoolhouse, the teenager soon conspired to purloin an extra meal. Ransacking the cabin, he discovered flour, lard and salt. He had seen his mother and sister fashion short cake from those ingredients, so, rolling up his sleeves, he mixed the flour with water, laced in lard and a couple pinches of salt, then kneaded it thoroughly. Placing the unleavened mixture in a spider, as pioneers called the long-

48

handled frying pans indispensable to their cookery, he laid it over glowing embers in the fireplace.

Just then came a rap on the door. Frightened at being caught dough-handed while preparing his unauthorized repast, he opened the door a crack to explain to the visitor that the family was away and he was busy mixing up chicken feed.

Suddenly, the shrill squawking of a rooster startled Van Buren. Turning, he saw the bird standing in the middle of his cake, beak full of dough, wings flapping and "yelping like murder" as the hot spider burned its feet. The visitor took in the situation at a glance and bid adieu, chuckling as he left. Van Buren yanked the bird out of the pan by the neck, threw him outside, carefully cut out the middle of the fowled cake, finishing cooking what was left and made of it a square meal. "Appetite always keen, but now heightened as stolen apples are sweetest," he wrote, "I relished the cake exceedingly," leaving not a crumb as a clue to his deed.

That culinary adventure punctuated the tedium of pork and potatoes for one meal and potatoes and pork for the next. The prevalence on the Michigan frontier of the tuber made famous by the Irish came in large part through the efforts of Kalamazoo's founder, Titus Bronson. Emigrating from Connecticut to Ohio in the early 1820's, he encountered a new superior variety of potato called the Neshannock. Bronson began cultivating them as a market crop for which he received a good price. The restless entrepreneur moved to Oakland County, then to the Ann Arbor vicinity in 1824 where his zeal for the starchy roots earned him the nickname Potato Bronson. After he first settled the site of Kalamazoo in 1829, the Johnny Appleseed of spuds spread the crop to the region's fertile oak openings.

The pioneer's pork supply came salted down in barrels and laboriously imported from eastern markets or butchered, scalded, scraped and preserved through smoking, salting or pickling by the frontiersmen them-

Pioneer cooks had little to work with but still managed
to prepare delicious meals.

selves. Hogs tended to be the "razorback" variety, long-legged, long-bodied, long-nosed, short-eared and nasty-tempered creatures popularly called "elm peelers" or "wind splitters." Turned loose in the woods to forage on acorns, roots, rattlesnakes and anything else they might sniff out, the feral porkers had to be hunted like wild game.

While it lasted, Michigan's bounteous wild life also formed an important part of the pioneer diet. Many frontiersmen became skilled hunters of deer, turkey, bear, rabbits and squirrels. The discovery of immense passenger pigeon roosts sometimes proved providential in getting pioneer families through the hard early years.

Those lucky enough to have led a cow or a nanny goat alongside their Conestoga wagons enjoyed the luxury of milk, butter and cheese. That is, until the animal wandered away in the unfenced wilderness or was tortured to death by clouds of gnats, mosquitoes and deer flies. Should the standard beast of burden, the ox, injure itself or grow too old to pull its weight, the family enjoyed a rare treat of beef.

But even with meat and potatoes plentiful, pioneers considered it a poor meal without "the staff of life." Before the initial wheat crops could be harvested, packing expensive barrels of flour to remote cabins proved a difficult proposition. Harriet Noble, who pioneered with her husband and large brood of children in the Dexter area in 1824, recalled going without flour for long periods. She wrote: "After being without bread three or four days, my little boy, two years old, looked me in the face and said, 'Ma, why can't you make bread; don't you like it? I do.' His innocent complaint brought forth the first tears I had shed in Michigan on account of my privations."

But even with flour available, pioneers often lacked yeast or some other leavening agent. They improvised with a variety of odoriferous substitutes including "salt risings" and "milk emptins," which relied on the fermentation of a mixture of salt water or salted milk. Caroline Kirkland, a sophisticated New Yorker who found herself transplated to the rough and tumble Livingston County frontier of the 1830s, thought "the sin of bewitching snow-white flour by means of those abominations ought to be classed with turning grain into whiskey, and both made indictable offenses."

Milling the wheat might also pose a problem. Van Buren recalled that when some unexpected visitors arrived at their cabin his mother had nothing but a couple quarts of wheat in the house. The resourceful woman had him grind the wheat in a pepper mill, and she prepared a delicious graham-flour shortcake of the unbolted product.

Other pioneers fashioned primitive tools to manufacture corn meal. Some ground it by hand between two rocks, Indian fashion, or grated the grain by rubbing it over a strip of tin punched with rough-edged holes. Ann Arbor pioneers developed a more ingenious technology. Sarah Bryan, who settled there in 1823, remembered the thumping echoes of the corn mills each morning. After burning a hole in the top of an oak stump and dumping in a peck of corn, they pounded it with a stick, six feet long and eight inches in diameter, suspended from a spring pole. A diligent miller could pound into meal a peck of corn in half an hour.

Pioneers relished their corn meal as corn dodger, which was meal, water and salt mixed into a stiff dough ball and baked in a covered iron pot buried in hot coals. Others favored corn pone, a richer mixture containing milk and leavening that rose into a big loaf, or johnny cake, which was meal mixed with lard, bear grease or butter and baked flat on a wooden board. Some savored steaming bowls of corn meal mush,

"Indian pudding" or cold mush fried and topped with maple syrup or honey.

With "store bought" sugar practically unknown on the frontier, pioneers soon learned the virtues of natural sweeteners. They traded from the Indians mococks of maple sugar. After the natives had been driven west on their trail of tears, they tapped trees to produce sugar and syrup themselves. Other frontiersmen grew adept at "bee hunting," the art of tracking the insects to a honey-filled "bee tree." Seventeen-year-old Amanda McClelland, who settled in Hastings in 1837, thought she had done well by trading a batch of nice clear honey from the Indians camped along the Thornapple River. That is, until she later discovered they had strained it through a filthy old blanket. "We did not eat any more honey after that," she recorded.

Early Michigan settlers also learned to fashion substitutes for other viands they craved. At festive events they steeped the leaves of a wild plant called tea-weed or quaffed cups of crust coffee made from toasted grains of wheat. Lacking cucumbers, they pickled crocks of green corn stalks sliced in appropriate shape. New Englanders who longed for seafood delicacies concocted mock oysters of a deep-fried mixture of egg, grated sweet corn and milk. And those who missed the raising of a social glass or two brewed a hearty beer of princess pine, winter-green, squawberries and sassafras roots, boiled, strained, sweetened and fermented in a wooden tub.

Despite the monotony of frontier cookery, the lack of seasonings and the Michigan appetite that griped many a belly, old pioneers affectionately remembered those simple meals of platters heaped high with boiled potatoes, fried pork, bowls of thick flour gravy and great crumbling chunks of johnny cake.

Something seems to have been lost when the railroads snaked across the state to bring eastern delicacies again within reach. Writing in the 1880s, Van Buren felt those pioneer foods were "eaten and relished more than the sumptuous meals on many of our tables now-a-days."

"Tell me what a people eat and I will tell you their morals," he quoted. "The old pioneer bill of fare was simple and wholesome, its morals can easily be deduced. What shall we say of the modern bill of fare?"

Benjamin F. Taylor, who taught school in Michigan during the pioneer era, included an engraving of a comely country maiden churning butter in his *Songs of Yesterday.*

Charles Lanman, Michigan's First Native-Born Author of Distinction

Charles Lanman was feeling blue one summer's day in 1841. Working long hours indoors as a New York City merchant's clerk, in a metropolis where pedestrians insensitive to strangers thronged the sidewalks, the 21-year-old pined for the friendly place where he had spent his first 15 wonderful years. The homesick youth dipped a quill in the ink bottle and scratched out: "Memory is telling me of my childhood's home, the dearest and most lovely spot on the face of the earth, and I regret I can visit it only in my dreams."

Lanman paused, as he thought about that home, a large frame dwelling on the bank of the River Raisin on the south side of Front Street in the ancient French village of Monroe, where he had been born on June 14, 1819. Then dipping his pen again and again, he warmed to his theme, filling the foolscap before him:

It is telling me the thrilling legends which fascinated my boyish imagination, where, with my bow and arrow, and clad in my hunting garb, I visited the Indian villages of Michigan. The better I have ever become acquainted with the red man of the wilderness, the more deeply have I loved him, and the more highly have I honored his character, and I regret that I cannot now, as of yore, chase with him the bounding deer, and paddle the light canoe... Memory is telling me of those matchless lakes, Superior, Michigan, Huron and Erie, whose every inlet almost I have explored, and from many of whose cliffs I have watched the most glorious of sunsets... Of those rivers too, the Detroit, the St. Clair, the St. Joseph, the Huron and the Raisin, in whose transparent waters I have often caught the sturgeon, the pickerel, and the bass, and along

*whose borders I have often hunted the plover and
the duck. Of those glorious forests, the homes of
solitude and silence, where I was wont to be happy
beyond compare. Of those prairies, boundless and
beautiful, for which the speech of England has no
name, where I wandered in dreamy mood, gather-
ing the richest of flowers, with which to adorn the
neck and forelock of my favorite steed.*

And then, suddenly, his reverie ended - the rhap-
sody was over, disturbed perhaps by the busy clatter in
the street outside. Looking around at his home away
from home Lanman sighed as he wrote: "I regret that it
is my lot to live so far removed from all these things
which are fast passing away, and that my pursuits com-
pel me to live in a world of mere business and fashion."

Alas, Lanman, like many another Michigander,
would be forced to follow his star, resulting in a long
and illustrious career as a writer, artist, librarian and in
government service, far removed from his beloved
home state. But as he pursued his life work and established himself as Michigan's first native-born author of
distinction, he would return time and again to Michigan
for themes that would promote and celebrate those
majestic peninsulas.

His father, Charles James Lanman, figures
prominently in the annals of the community originally
called Frenchtown but renamed Monroe in 1817 by
Territorial Governor Lewis Cass in honor of President
James Monroe's visit to the territory. A native of
Connecticut, following graduation from Yale College
and admittance to the bar, the elder Lanman took the
advice of his friends Cass and Territorial Secretary
William Woodbridge and cast his lot with Michigan.
Settling in Monroe in 1817, Lanman would serve as
attorney for the territory, judge of probate, militia
colonel, customs inspector, postmaster and receiver of
money for the federal land office. He co-founded

Tecumseh and served on a commission that designated the county seats of Ionia, Kent and Clinton counties. The illness of his parents drew him back to Connecticut in 1835 and during his absence the effects of the Financial Panic of 1837 brought about the loss of most of his Michigan property, thus severing his ties to the state.

Son Charles, one of nine siblings born to Lanman and his French Canadian wife, Marie Jeanne Gruie, enjoyed an idyllic youth in Monroe. His writings preserve childhood memories of playmates, sons of some of the great men who were making Michigan history: Cass, Woodbridge and Henry Rowe Schoolcraft. He enjoyed friendships with those men as well. Decades later he would publish a biography of Woodbridge. He also had the pleasure of introducing Schoolcraft to the publisher who produced his monumental six-volume set of Indian lore.

But during his days in Monroe, Lanman's real love lay in the pristine woods and rivers rather than the politics, legal proceedings and the affairs of state which occupied his father. He spent a "wild and wayward boyhood" as recorded in an autobiographical essay first published in 1841 and later expanded and refined in several other books:

> *In the prime of summer I have watched for pigeons on the margins of the forest springs, or waded the streams after the sweet crawfish; in the strangely beautiful autumn and Indian summer I have captured the squirrel and partridge; and in the winter the turkey and deer. Reader have you ever, while roaming in the woods bordering a prairie, startled from his heathery couch a noble buck, and seen him dart from you 'swift as an arrow from a shivering bow.' Was it not a sight worthy of a purer world than ours?*

Scattered among his other writings, Lanman recorded numerous childhood adventures, while hunting deer, ducks and wolves, being lost in the woods and rescued by an Indian, monumental snow ball fights, horse races along the frozen river, merry sleigh rides to dances and fishing forays on the River Raisin and the St. Joseph River near Niles. Once he speared a monster sturgeon and rode the leviathan Hiawatha-like down the River Raisin.

Perhaps because he eschewed the schoolroom for the thrill of the chase, Lanman, by his own admission, had been "classed as one who would never amount to anything." And judging from his numerous later references to the glory of his youth in Michigan he may well have been content to spend the remainder of his life roaming those beautiful forests and streams. But parental fiat sealed his fate. The youth was banished from his beloved Michigan to stay with his grandfather. For the next five years he chafed under the tuteladge of strict pedagogues in an academy at Plainfield, Connecticut. Most biographical references claim Lanman left Michigan at the age of ten but he, himself, wrote that he spent the first 15 years of his life in the territory. Perhaps he returned for long summers and holiday vacations as it seems unlikely that a ten-year-old could have garnered the extensive Michigan experiences he recorded.

In any event, after graduation from the academy, roughly equivalent to a high school degree, Lanman took a position as clerk in a New York City-based East India trading firm. Over the succeeding decade, he worked long hours indoors, persevering and advancing to an executive position with the company. But he continued to yearn for Michigan, as expressed in the pages of his first book published in 1841, *Essays for Summer Hours*.

That volume included as a frontispiece an oval

engraving of an Indian canoeing on a wilderness river drawn by Lanman. During his stint in New York Lanman had taken up the study of engraving and painting under Asher B. Durand, a leading landscape painter of the Hudson River School of Art. Elected an associate of the prestigious National Academy of Design in 1846, Lanman would pursue a long and fruitful avoca-

Charles Lanman never lost his love for the sport of fishing that he learned as a boy in Monroe.

tion as an artist that would rival his literary efforts.

Lanman's second book, *Letters from a Landscape Painter*, appeared in 1845. That year Lanman responded to the pull of his home state. Returning to Monroe, he edited the Monroe *Gazette*. That reconciliation lasted but a few months, however, and he advanced to a position as associate editor of the Cincinnati *Chronicle*.

The summer of 1846 found Lanman embarking on an epic canoe trip up the Mississippi River, along the southern shore of Lake Superior and down Lake Huron, with a obligatory sojourn at Sault Ste. Marie and Mackinac Island, before returning to Monroe. He recorded the events of that journey, including colorful description of voyageurs, the torments of mosquitos, the Keweenaw copper rush, fishing in the St. Marys Rapids and other Michigan adventures, in *A Summer in the Wilderness* (1847). Incidently, the colorful copper boom then in progress impressed Lanman but little. He thought the majority of those who had swarmed to the Keweenaw Peninsula "dishonest speculators and inexperienced adventurers."

By the time of the appearance of Lanman's third book, he had returned to New York City where he wrote for the *Daily Express*. The following year he visited Washington, D.C., married Adeline Dodge and settled in Georgetown. There he made his living as a traveling correspondent for the *National Intelligencer*. The letters and articles he wrote about his numerous trips and sporting adventures became books: *A Tour to the River Saguenay* (1848), *Letters From the Alleghaney Mountains* (1849) and *Haw-Ho-Noo, or Records of a Tourist* (1850). Haw-Ho-Noo, Iroquois for America, had been suggested as a title by his old friend Schoolcraft. The volume contains 26 varied Indian legends Lanman had collected during his western rambles, including several by Michigan

Chippewa and Potawatomi storytellers. In 1856, Lanman republished his seven books of travel in two fat volumes, *Adventures in the Wilds of America.*

In the meantime, his career had taken even more of a bookish focus. He served successively as librarian of the War Department, of copyrights in the State Department, of the Interior Department and of the House of Representatives. Any good librarian, then as now, savors reference demands and Lanman saw the need for a succinct biographical guide to congressmen. He compiled the *Dictionary of the United States Congress* in 1859. A classic work, it went through six revised editions and formed the basis of a much expanded version Lanman first published in 1876, *Biographical Annals of the Civil Government of the United States.*

Lanman compiled his biographies from research in government archives and from questionnaires he distributed to subjects. As opposed to rather lengthy accounts of Stephen A. Douglas, Jefferson Davis and other leading politicos of the period, the terse 1859 biography of the man who would be elected president the following year, taken from a handwritten reply he had furnished Lanman, remains a model of humility:

Lincoln, Abraham
He was born in Hardin County, Kentucky, February 12, 1809; received a limited education; adopted the profession of law; was a captain of volunteers in the Black Hawk War; at one time postmaster of a small village; four times elected to the Illinois legislature; and a Representative in Congress from Illinois, from 1847 to 1849.

Lanman would later become a personal friend to Lincoln as well as other important figures of the times, including William Cullen Bryant, Henry Wadsworth

Longfellow, Washington Irving, Henry Clay, Horace Greeley, and Daniel Webster. For two years, beginning in 1850, Lanman served as Webster's private secretary and, based on their intimate relationship, he wrote *The Private Life of Daniel Webster* in 1852.

As the century wore on and Lanman moved from one profession to another, he took on the quality of a renaissance man. Each new endeavor inspired additional books. In 1867, he paid homage to his childhood friend with *The Life of William Woodbridge*. Four years later, he followed in the steps of his uncle, James Lanman, who had published the first full scale history of Michigan in 1839, with *The Red Book of Michigan*, a massive, historical and biographical compilation, chronicling primarily the state's role in the Civil War.

In 1871, Lanman became the first American secretary to the Japanese legation in Washington, a position he would hold until 1882. Three books flowed from that new career: *The Resources of America*, compiled for the Japanese government in 1872; *The Japanese in America* (1872); and *Leading Men of Japan* (1883).

In 1882, Lanman left public employment to concentrate on painting and writing. In 1885, he published *Farthest North,* a biography of James Booth Lockwood, who perished along with Edward Israel from Kalamazoo and 16 other members of the ill-fated Greely Arctic Expedition. Lanman's last book, *Haphazard Personalities* (1886), contains information about Cass, Schoolcraft and other Michigan figures unavailable elsewhere. Prior to his death on March 4, 1895, he completed an estimated 1,000 works of art and 32 books. He lies next to his wife Adeline, his companion on several wilderness canoe trips, in Washington's Oakhill Cemetery.

No more fitting epitaph for the Michigan boy

who made good can be found than the words he penned in his first book more than a half century before his death:

> *O Michigan! "thou art my own, my native land," and I love thee tenderly. Thy skies are among the most gorgeous, - thy soil the most luxuriant, - thy birds and flowers the most beautiful; — and thy animals the most interesting in the world. And when I remember that thou art but a single volume in His library, and that these things are the hand-writing of God, my affection for thee becomes more strong. I believe thou art destined to be distinguished and honored by the nations of the earth, God be with thee, and crown thee with his blessing!*

Charles Lanman's beloved birthplace in Monroe.

The Saga of the Ontonagon Boulder

For untold centuries the mysterious gleaming boulder, mottled with green patina, studded the shore of the rushing Ontonagon River some 25 miles upstream from where its waters mingled with Lake Superior. The native Chippewa revered its shining presence as a gift from Gitchi Manitou. The Jesuit fathers who first carried the cross to the Upper Peninsula wilderness wrote back letters to France describing the huge nugget of native copper. Succeeding generations of explorers hacked souvenir chunks from its bulk. Eighteenth-century British adventurers and 19th-century American expeditions labored vainly to retrieve the three-ton monolith. Finally, the vision, determination and pluck of a feisty Detroit shopkeeper secured the prize, but only to have it wrenched away by covetous Washington officials.

As early as 500 B.C. prehistoric tribesmen had pocked primitive mines into the Upper Peninsula copper country, one of few places in the world containing large, pure nuggets of the red metal. When Jacques Cartier explored the St. Lawrence River in the 1530s the natives told him of the copper riches to the west. Shortly after Samuel de Champlain founded Quebec in 1608, the local Chippewa presented him with a slab of native copper, "a foot long, very handsome and quite pure," which came from the "bank of a great river flowing into a great lake" to the west. Champlain's explorer, Entienne Brule, who discovered Lake Superior in 1620, also returned with copper gifts.

But deposits of pure copper failed to stir much interest among the French, who saw more potential in the fur trade and pursuit of a water route across the continent to the fabled riches of the Orient. The French lost New France to the British in 1763, and three years later the first Englishman found his way to the already famous Ontonagon Boulder. Alexander Henry, best known for his thrilling escape from the massacre at Fort Michilimackinac, described it as "a mass of copper of the weight, according to my estimate, of no less than five tons. Such was its pure and malleable state that with an axe I was able to cut off a portion weighing one hundred pounds."

Henry returned to the site in 1771 with a party of Birmingham coal miners. After an aborted attempt to raise the copper boulder, the miners burrowed a 40-foot cavity in the adjacent clay bluff, groping for a copper and, hopefully, silver lode. But when the succeeding spring thaw caved in the tunnel, the miners retreated back to civilization unburdened with metallic riches.

In the summer of 1820, Michigan Territorial Governor Lewis Cass led a canoe expedition along the southern shore of Lake Superior. Chippewa braves from a village at the mouth of the Ontonagon guided Henry Rowe Schoolcraft, geologist of the expedition, up the river to the foot of a series of impassable rapids then overland across five miles of rugged terrain to the boulder. Schoolcraft found the rock disappointedly small, although the engraving he included in his travel narrative depicts it as large as a house. He estimated the copper portion of the boulder to weigh 2,200 pounds, noting that its size had shrunk due to "the marks of chisels and axes upon it, with the broken tools lying around."

When Schoolcraft attempted to further diminish its size by detaching specimens his "chisels broke like glass." Determined to secure samples, Cass sent a party of men back to the boulder the following spring. They succeeding in dragging the rock a few feet out of the current then piled on 30 cord of firewood. After the ensuing fire had burned down they dashed buckets of cold water against the rock to crack off sections. The big boulder stood impervious to the fiery ordeal.

The engraving of the Ontonagon Boulder Henry Rowe Schoolcraft included in his 1821 travel narrative depicts it as the size of a house!

Douglass Houghton and other geological explorers paid homage to the celebrated boulder. But even as Michigan entered the union in 1837 and was awarded the western two thirds of the Upper Peninsula in exchange for the Toledo Strip, the Ontonagon boulder, which had been hacked, gouged, cut, chipped, moved a little and fired to a red glow over nearly two centuries, remained adamantly *in situ*.

Then in 1841, a 53-year-old ex-banker, woolen manufacturer and hardware merchant from Detroit named Julius Eldred entered the saga. Galvanized by State Geologist Houghton's reports on the richness of the copper country and through conversations with Joseph Spence, who had been part of a botched attempt to retrieve the Ontonagon Boulder in 1826, Eldred determined to succeed where so many others had failed. He would bring the prize to Detroit and make his fortune by charging the public a fee to view the marvel.

One detail stood in his way. By the Treaty of 1826 the Chippewa had ceded to the U.S. government the right to remove minerals, but the Indians still legally owned the land. So when Eldred arrived at Sault Ste. Marie in early summer 1841, he secured a trading license from Indian Agent James Ord and hired Judge Samuel Ashman, an old fur trader, to accompany him as guide and interpreter. At the village near the mouth of the Ontonagon, Eldred purchased the copper boulder from Chief Okondokon for $255, $150 down and the remainder if he succeeded in getting the rock to Lake Superior. The work force he brought from the Sault, bolstered by Indians, succeeded in raising the 6,000 pound copper and rock matrix from the river bed. Unable to accomplish more that season, Eldred paid off his laborers and returned to Detroit.

The following summer's efforts brought no more success. Back in Detroit, Eldred borrowed capital from his three sons and ordered a railroad flat car, ample block and tackle and two sections of 25-foot portable track. While Eldred busied himself in preparation for his third attempt during the winter of 1842-43, the U.S. Senate ratified a treaty with the Chippewa that ceded to the government the copper country land including the Ontonagon River.

Immediately, a party of prospectors from Wisconsin headed by a Col. Hammond raced overland to lay claim to the copper boulder. At the same time another group from the east secured a mining permit from Secretary of War James M. Porter. Their representative, Col. White, reached the Ontonagon site in May 1843 to find Hammond's armed men guarding the bolder. Rather than fight, White simply sold his permit to the Wisconsin miners.

When Eldred arrived with his portable railroad a few weeks later, he encountered a feisty set of Badger rogues camped around the boulder, unwilling to recognize the validity of the bargain he had made with the Chippewa chief in 1841. Hammond, perhaps realizing the difficulty he faced in getting the boulder downstream, offered to sell his rights to it for $1,300. Eldred scrawled out a bank draft for the amount and Hammond set out on the 500 mile voyage to Detroit to cash it.

Free now to pursue his task in peace, Eldred and his 20 workers tackled the most difficult part of their project - to cut out and smooth a road bed through heavy timber-lined hills and chasms five miles around the rapids. Then they spent a week inching the boulder with a capstan to the top of the 50-foot cliff at the river's edge. After loading the mass onto the flat car, for more than a month they grunted, sweated and swore, pushing and pulling the car with tackle attached to trees up and down the ragged hills.

When the railroad car finally reached the foot of

the rapids, Eldred lowered the boulder onto a raft and floated it to the river's mouth. Waiting there was Hammond, mad as a hornet: the Detroit bank had refused to honor Eldred's draft, and he wanted his boulder back. Eldred assured him that he would get the cash and reimburse him for his 1,000-mile travel expenses, and he set sail for Detroit.

On his way back north with Hammond's money, Eldred chartered the schooner *Algonquin* to convey the boulder to Sault Ste. Marie. But when the schooner stopped at Copper Harbor, Walter Cunningham, the government mineral agent, handed Eldred a startling document: a directive from Secretary of War Porter ordering him "to seize the boulder in the name of the United States, and if necessary to call out the troops at Fort Brady."

In sympathy with Eldred's plight, Cunningham deputized him and allowed him to transport the boulder to Detroit while awaiting reimbursement from the government for his trouble and expense. At the mouth of the Ontonagon, Eldred paid Hammond $1,765 and Chief Okondokon $105 and loaded the copper rock aboard the *Algonquin*.

At the Sault, the boulder was portaged around the St. Marys Rapids and loaded on another vessel for the last leg of its journey to Detroit. When it arrived on October 11, 1843, displaying showmanship worthy of P.T. Barnum, Eldred had the rock draped in black and pulled by four black stallions from the landing to a gallery on Jefferson Avenue. Detroiters, including Schoolcraft who had last seen the rock 23 years before, soon queued up to pay 25¢ to view the marvelous mineral specimen.

Porter, however, egged on by officials of the precursor of the Smithsonian Institution, had no intention of allowing the prize to remain in Detroit. On November 1, the big boulder was loaded aboard a U.S.

revenue cutter and transported to Washington. Eldred applied to Congress for redress and after lengthy lobbying, in 1847 was finally awarded $5,664.98 for his amazing accomplishment. He died four years later.

Widespread publicity over the copper rock that had caused so much government consternation helped launch the Keweenaw copper rush which presaged the 49'ers scramble for California gold.

Once in federal hands, the boulder sat in the yard of the War Department, then on the grounds of the Patent Office until transferred to the U.S. National Museum in 1858. It lay forgotten in a dusty storeroom until a campaign by Alfred Mears, editor of the Ontonagon *Miner,* resulted in its placement on exhibit in the Smithsonian Institution in 1881. There, despite repeated attempts to return it to Michigan, the celebrated copper boulder from Ontonagon remains.

Prior to completion of the first lock, the Lake Superior shipping depot at Sault St. Marie resembled this 1852 print.

Caroline Quarreles'
Flight to Freedom

Titball, the black barber, was a rogue - worse, a Judas. And in 1842, as Caroline Quarreles made a flight for freedom via the underground railroad that stretched across southern Michigan, Titball would be one of several who taught the teenager that a person's skin hue held little clue to the color of the heart that beat within.

Caroline's great-great grandfather, a white man, had emigrated from Connecticut to Virginia where he married an Indian woman. At some point over the succeeding generations, African-American blood entered the family genealogy, and in the ante bellum south that usually resulted in the stain of slavery. Her father ended up in St. Louis where, about 1826, Caroline was born. Known as an octoroon, with one-eighth or less African lineage, Caroline grew into a pretty light-skinned teenager. Her long, dark tresses were her particular pride.

Following her parents' deaths, in a convoluted twist of fate Caroline became the property of her father's sister who had married Charles R. Hall, a St. Louis merchant. Although quite intelligent, Caroline was not taught to read or write, but rather was trained to sew, embroider and serve her aunt as a house slave. While not particularly abused, by slave standards, infractions brought her several beatings. Her mistress grew angry one day and as punishment cut off her niece's beautiful braids. Caroline determined that the Fourth of July, 1842, would mark her own bid for independence.

Somehow she got her hands on $100 cash and some expensive jewelry. She threw a bundle of clothes out her window and, gaining permission from her mistress to visit a sick girlfriend, made a beeline for the wharf. There she purchased a ticket to Alton, Illinois, the site of a female academy, and boarded a Mississippi River steamboat. With skin no darker than many of the other girls en route to the school, and wearing rich jewelry, she passed.

But when the steamer docked at Alton, a sharp-eyed black man sized her up as a runaway slave. When she denied his accusation, he told her, "not to conceal the fact from him, as he was a friend to all fugitive slaves, and that it would not be safe for her to remain in Alton." He put her on a stagecoach bound for Milwaukee. She jolted along day and night until she reached that city.

Alighting from the stage, stiff and sore, she spied Titball, the black barber, who operated a fancy shop in the Milwaukee House. Thinking that he would prove a friend like the man in Alton, she pled her plight. Taking her under his wing, in honeyed tones he told how he himself was an ex-slave and scurried her away to his house.

In the meantime, a slave hound in the form of a St. Louis lawyer named Spencer, was sniffing hard on the trail. In an era when choice government land sold for $1.25 an acre, and a working man counted himself lucky to earn five cents an hour, Caroline's owner valued her at $2,000. Her aunt quickly posted a $300 reward for her capture. Within a week after Caroline's arrival in Milwaukee, Spencer had traced her there.

It didn't take him long to ferret out Titball, who readily admitted giving Caroline sanctuary. While the lawyer dashed for reinforcements, the barber, who smelled an opportunity to make himself some money, dispatched a young ex-slave who worked for him to hide Caroline in a specified spot. Spencer linked up with a local pettifogger named J.E. Arnold. The pair searched Titball's house to no avail, whereupon the barber offered to surrender Caroline for $100.

They agreed, but when the traitor led them to the hiding place it was deserted. The boy employed by

Titball knew his boss's character only too well and had secreted Caroline in another location. The lawyers began ransacking Milwaukee for their quarry. That's when the local abolitionists came to the rescue.

Similar to the Wolverine State, the Badger State was largely pioneered by New Englanders who detested slavery. The Republican Party rose out of the anti-slavery movement in 1854 and it is no coincidence that Jackson, Michigan, and Ripon, Wisconsin, both lay claim as the birth place of the "grand old party." Waukesha and Pewaukee, communities to the west of Milwaukee, were hot beds of abolitionists. That is where Samuel Brown, recognized as Wisconsin's first underground railroad conductor, spirited the teenager.

The underground railroad, an organized system to relay runaway slaves to Canada, where slavery had long been outlawed, was largely the work of Quakers. Levi Coffin, a Cincinnati Quaker, established an Ohio underground railroad network in 1840. That same year, John Cross, a Hoosier Quaker, laid out a spur across southern Michigan. There, over the succeeding two decades, thousands of black fugitives received support and shelter during their trek to Canada.

Underground railroad routes from Indiana and Illinois converged at the Quaker settlement in Cass County's Calvin Township. Zachariah Shugart operated the station there and Parker Osborn served as the agent at nearby Cassopolis. In Schoolcraft, the residence of Dr. Nathan Thomas and wife Pamela, now a museum, harbored more than 1,000 runaway slaves prior to the Civil War. William Gardner, Isaac Davis, Isaac Pierce and other conductors lived in Climax, known by slave hunters as an "abolition hole." Erastus Hussey operated one of Michigan's busiest stations in Battle Creek. Other documented stations existed in Marshall, Albion, Parma, Jackson, Michigan Center, Leoni, Grass Lake, Dexter, Scio, and Ann Arbor. At Ypsilanti, the underground railroad veered north to

Plymouth and then skirted the River Rouge via Swartsburg to Detroit.

As the slave-hunting lawyers narrowed the chase for Caroline, and with no assistance available through the legal system because of the Fugitive Slave Act of 1793, the Wisconsin abolitionists determined to send the girl to Canada on the underground railroad. They chose Lyman Goodnow, a bachelor, as the conductor.

Titball had already relieved Caroline of her money. Cash was scarce on the frontier, but the abolitionists chipped in whatever they could spare to speed the two on "their visit to the Queen." They set off in a buggy on the 600-mile circuitous route that wound south to Illinois, Indiana and across Michigan. Traveling first only under cover of darkness, they found food and shelter at the underground railroad sta-

This, the only known picture of Caroline Quarreles, appeared in a rare genealogy published in 1893.

tions that lay 15 to 20 miles apart.

Near Laporte, Indiana, a raging storm prevented them from reaching the next station. They sought refuge at a claim shanty occupied by a German couple. The settler told Goodnow, "We have no bed for you, no fire, no wood and no candles, but will gladly give you a place of shelter." Caroline quickly crawled into bed with the *frau* and Goodnow stretched out on the floor with their host. The travelers were up and away before dawn, and the hospitable Germans never suspected they had abetted a runaway slave.

Crossing into Michigan, the fugitives traveled for three days among the Quakers of Berrien and Cass counties who invariably told them, "Thee can have what thee wants."

After leaving the Quaker settlements, they stopped over night at a house about five miles from Climax. Caroline hung her purse containing jewelry and the few dollars she had been given on a spinning wheel. In their haste to get an early start the next morning she forget it, and the loss was not discovered for 20 miles. Goodnow determined to push on and retrieve the valuables on his return trip.

As they continued east, traffic on the underground railroad grew brisk. Between Battle Creek and Marshall they encountered a gang of 32 escaped slaves boldly traveling by day.

Caroline and Goodnow reached the final station in Detroit three weeks after they had left Wisconsin. The agent there secured them a boat ride across the Detroit River and soon Caroline was "free at last!"

Suddenly, in confusion, she began sobbing and, clutching Goodnow's arm, pleading that he not take her back to her mistress: to Caroline the Detroit River banks appeared just like the Mississippi River opposite St. Louis. Goodnow at last convinced her she had not been betrayed and left her in the care of a Windsor missionary named Haskell.

Retracing his route back to Wisconsin, Goodnow stopped at the underground railroad station near Climax to retrieve Caroline's jewelry, but the wretched station master refused to return the purse. After lengthy argument Goodnow got him to agree to give up the jewelry if ample security was given.

Goodnow rode to Climax to get a bond signed by Dr. Stephen Thayer, who he knew to be a staunch abolitionist. The physician was away on his lonely horseback rounds, but after much trouble and several days' delay, Thayer readily wrote out an obligation.

Still, the "mean-souled individual" refused to give up the valuables. Fifty years later, Goodnow remembered: "I was terribly exasperated, but talked as coolly as I could until the purse was recovered, when I gave him as much deserved abuse as I could command, and I wish I could recall his name now, that the world might know what kind of men inscrutable Providence has from time to time permitted to live in it."

When he reached Wisconsin, Goodnow forwarded Caroline her possessions.

Goodnow continued as an active agent on the underground railroad over the succeeding two decades. He knew nothing of Caroline's subsequent life until 1880 when she sent him a letter. Three years after arriving in Canada, she had married an ex-slave named Watkins, and gave birth to three daughters and three sons. Caroline spent the remainder of her life in the country that had opened its arms to herself and thousands of other African-Americans at a time when their own nation was not genuinely "the land of the free."

When Doomsday Came & Went

Daniel B. Eldred, the pioneer who bestowed on Climax its distinctive name, set out from his farm on the prairie for Kalamazoo one morning in October 1844. As he neared Galesburg one of his wagon wheels began to wobble. He had lost the linchpin that kept it from slipping off the axle. Eldred pulled up before a blacksmith shop to get a new pin fitted. The artisan soon hammered out the pin, tried it for size and found it a trifle large. He was about to file it down when Eldred said, "Drive it in, it will answer for three days. I shan't want it after that as the world is coming to an end."

The blacksmith pounded in the pin "so tight that an ox-team could not have drawn it out," and Eldred resumed his trip, loudly proclaiming to all he met, "the end of the world is at hand."

Eldred fervently believed that October 22, 1844, marked the Millennium - "court week in heaven." Christ would appear in the sky, the righteous rise from the grave and ascend with the living righteous heavenward as the sinful world was destroyed by fire. And he was not alone in that conviction - across America several hundred thousand believers, including many in Michigan, anxiously awaited Judgement Day. The followers of the teachings of an upper New York state farmer-turned-preacher named William Miller became known as Millerites.

The man who launched this apocalyptic furor had spent the early part of his life as anything but a rabble-rouser. Born in Pittsfield, Massachusetts, in 1782, the eldest of 16 siblings, Miller grew up on a farm near the hamlet of Low Hampton, New York, north of Albany near the Vermont border. His stern Baptist parents allowed only three books in the home, a bible, a psalter and a hymnal. Yet young Miller parleyed his meager education of three months schooling each win-

77

William Miller created quite a commotion when he predicted the imminent end of the world.

ter into a love of learning. Abraham Lincoln-like he chopped wood for books and borrowed volumes on ancient history from neighbors. By the age of 15 he had gained local fame as "scribbler-general," drafting letters and verse for his less literate companions.

Miller married in 1803, settling six miles to the east in Poultney, Vermont. In that town's library he fell under the sway of the heretical writings of Voltaire, Thomas Paine and others. He joined the ranks of the deists, who in reaction to the prevalent fundamentalism of the era believed that after creating the world a Supreme Being had exercised no further interference in the orderly laws of nature.

Despite his unorthodox beliefs, Miller led the life of an exemplary citizen. He served as town constable, won election as deputy sheriff of the county and rose in rank in the local militia unit. As a captain in the regular army he fought bravely in the War of 1812.

Miller returned to civilian life as a farmer near Low Hampton. But his military experiences had left him both "completely disgusted with man's public character" and thirsting for some greater meaning to his own being. That meaning came as a flash while listening to a sermon in the local Baptist Church in 1816. Renouncing deism, he became a church stalwart. Bible study became his passion as he burned the midnight oil scrutinizing the scriptures. The arcane verses of Daniel and Revelations, in particular, struck his fancy. Miller puzzled over those passages for two years, discerning a consistent thread pointing toward "the destruction of the world and its wicked, unbelieving inhabitants at the Second Coming of Christ." Further perusal yielded the master key that unlocked the biblical symbolism to reveal the precise date of the cataclysm. Miller tested his computations 15 different ways and in each case got the same result - 1843.

Miller kept his mathematical masterpiece to himself until, finally, in 1831, he felt compelled to tell the world. He began preaching his frightening doctrine a hundred or more times a year while traveling throughout the eastern states. Disciples carried the word to the west and the Millerites garnered converts by the thousands.

The Reverend Moses Clark, a Baptist minister who preached the first sermon in Ann Arbor in 1825,

A spectacular meteor shower in 1833 seemed to portend
Miller's dire prophecies.

caught the millennial fever in the early 1840s. He held a series of meetings at the Climax schoolhouse which doubled as the community's Baptist Church, creating "a tremendous excitement" among the settlers who traveled many miles to pack the log structure. Elder Joseph Byron, an eccentric Methodist from Climax who had once dashed the entire contents of a baptismal font on a parishioner's head for requesting to be baptized by pouring rather than sprinkling, also began "preaching the speedy end of the world" to all who would listen.

As the time drew neigh, unusual meteorological and astronomical phenomena seemed to many to portend Miller's accuracy. Deadly tornadoes, a spectacular meteor shower in 1833 and a sublime display of the Aurora Borealis in 1837 brought increased consternation. Then in March 1843, the most brilliant comet of the century flashed across the heavens, clearly visible even at midday.

Miller had not predicted the exact date of the apocalypse, simply that it would occur sometime within the year that, based on the ancient Jewish Calendar, ended on March 21, 1844.

As that final day approached Millerites across the nation prepared for the end. Some simply put their affairs in order, paid off all debts and smugly awaited their "going up." Others abandoned their professions, left fields unplowed and crops unharvested. Some few stitched white cambric ascension robes for the big event. Children quit attending school - what was the use? One young boy asked his mother why they couldn't kill all the chickens and turkeys and have one final grand feast? On March 21st, Ascension Day, some Millerites climbed nearby hills or gathered in cemeteries to watch the resurrection of their loved ones.

The day following the "Great Disappointment" dawned on a sect somewhat embarrassed but steadfast in its views. Miller recalculated and came up with October 22, 1844, as the correct date. Once again fields lay fallow and chores neglected. Some Millerites grew hysterical, spoke in tongues, danced the holy dance and laughed the holy laugh.

Many of Miller's followers took the second "Great Disappointment" pretty hard. Eldred, who had been financially ruined by the fiasco, sold his run-down Climax farm and moved with his family to Virginia.

But a stubborn coterie of Millerites worked out an explanation for the humiliation - Miller's computations were correct, but his error lay in his interpretation of what was to happen. Make no mistake, the end was still near, but the exact date remained a mystery.

Out of the wreckage of the Millerite movement, augmented by the doctrine that Saturday ought to be celebrated as the Sabbath and bolstered by the prophetic visions of a 17-year-old Maine farm girl named Ellen G. Harmon, evolved the Seventh Day Adventist Church.

Harmon married another Millerite zealot, James White, and in 1855 they moved to Battle Creek. Over the succeeding half century Battle Creek emerged as the headquarters of the faith. There, the Adventists operated Michigan's largest printing plant to churn out the millions of tracts that proselytized its tenets throughout the world.

A century and a half after the "epidemic mass delusion" of the Millerites, a supposedly more sophisticated America witnessed the tragic end of David Koresh's Branch Davidians. The appearance of comet Hale-Bop inspired the mass suicide of 39 members of the Heaven's Gate cult. And some 140 Taiwanese followers of God's Salvation Church in the Dallas, Texas, suburb of Garland awaited the descent of God from Heaven on March 31, 1998.

Testy Trollope's Travels

It was a bright moonlit night in October 1861, when celebrated British novelist Anthony Trollope set out on an after-dinner constitutional to look over Grand Haven. The fine meal he had enjoyed aboard the steamer scheduled to transport him across Lake Michigan to Milwaukee of "beefsteaks, and tea, and apple jam, and hot cakes, and light fixings," had, unfortunately, done little to sooth his irascible nature. It did not take him long to brand the second busiest port on Lake Michigan "a more melancholy place I never beheld." "Altogether," Trollope mercilessly concluded in his travel narrative published in 1862, "it is a dreary place, such as might break a man's heart, should he find that inexorable fate required him there to pitch his tent."

One of a long line of peevish British literary travelers who found little to like in America, Trollope seemed intent on emulating his mother's scathing account of frontier culture, *Domestic Manners of the Americans,* published 30 years before. Trollope's mother Frances and father Thomas, a nere-do-well barrister who frittered away the family fortune through repeated blunders, had immigrated to Cincinnati in 1828. There they constructed an "architectural monstrosity" dubbed the "Bazaar" and launched in ill-fated scheme to merchandise imported British goods. Two years later, the Trollopes retreated back to England, bankrupt again.

Realizing that if her family was to escape the poor house it was up to her, at the age of 50 and never having written anything for publication before, Frances began a book about her American experiences. Published in 1832, her vivid portrayal of American society, which she perceived as "rough, uncouth and vulgar," became an immediate best seller. Her descriptions of patrons at a Cincinnati theatre who hung their feet over the gallery, for example, for decades gave rise to the pejorative cry "Trollope!" at anyone who committed a similar offense.

Smarting at her criticisms, perhaps because they were not entirely amiss, American writers howled in protest. During the 1830s, as literary historian Ralph Rusk noted, "No other English writer, with the exception of Scott and Byron, was as well known throughout the West and none so sordidly hated." Mrs. Trollope stayed on her side of the Atlantic for the remaining 31 years of her life, becoming an enormously prolific author of European travel books and novels, immensely popular and rich.

Her son Anthony, born in 1815, suffered a miserable childhood. A "large awkward boy, ill clad and often dirty," he was cruelly ostracized by the young aristocrats with whom he was forced to attend private school. At the age of 19 he secured a job as a junior clerk with the post office and spent the following seven years in lonely, dingy poverty in London. Fortune eventually smiled on him in 1841 when he was promoted and transferred to Ireland. Finally financially at ease, he lost his shyness, took up fox hunting and three years later married the daughter of a local banker.

Dismayed by the Irish discontent he witnessed, he set out to learn the genuine reasons for the ethnic hatred. He turned his research into two unsuccessful political novels published in 1847 and 1848. He persevered and ultimately found his metier as a master at describing the intricacies of British ecclesiastical and middle class social life. By 1861 he had written ten novels, including his best remembered, *Barchester Towers* (1857), and enjoyed a popular following. In the meantime he had won continued promotion in the post office, traveling extensively on postal missions. In 1859, he moved to a suburb of London.

Trollope applied for a leave of absence from the post office in 1861 to accomplish "the ambition of my

Cantankerous Anthony Trollope found little to like in Michigan.

literary life to write a book about the United States." He determined not to allow the Civil War that broke out in April 1861 to interfere with his plans. In August, he and wife Rose sailed from Liverpool to Boston. After touring New England, the Trollopes visited Ontario and Niagara Falls and then traveled by rail to Windsor.

Boarding the Detroit ferry, Trollope and a hundred other passengers, "at once sat down to breakfast" before landing at the "City of the Straits." It did not take the cantankerous Brit long to size up Detroit, and he was no kinder in his description of that city of 70,000 inhabitants than he would be of Grand Haven:

> I have not much to say of Detroit; not much, that is, beyond what I have to say of all the North. It is a large well-built half-finished city, lying on a convenient water way, and spreading itself out with promises of a wide and still wider prosperity. It has about it perhaps as little of intrinsic interest as any of those large western towns which I visited. It is not so pleasant as Milwaukee, nor so picturesque as St. Paul, nor so grand as Chicago, nor so civilized as Cleveland, nor so busy as Buffalo. Indeed Detroit is neither pleasant nor picturesque at all. I will not say it is uncivilized, but it has a harsh, crude, unprepossessing appearance. I do not think it well to recommend any Englishman to make a special visit to Detroit, who may be wholly uncommercial in his views and travel in search of that which is either beautiful or interesting.

The Trollopes booked passage on the Detroit and Milwaukee Railroad which extended through Pontiac, Durand and Grand Rapids to Grand Haven. As the train clicked along the rails, Trollope was amazed at how "absolutely wild" the scenery appeared.

"For miles upon miles," he wrote, "the road passes the untouched forest, showing that even in Michigan the great work of civilization has hardly more than been commenced." Trollope imagined the vast acreage tamed and "the crowds which will grow sleek and talk loudly, and become aggressive on these wheat and meat producing levels."

After describing the geography of the peninsulas for his British readers, Trollope let slip the only compliment he would grant Michigan: "I doubt whether any large inland territory in the world be blessed with such facilities of water carriage."

When the British tourists reached Grand Haven, they found the big black-hulled steamer port-bound due to a storm on Lake Michigan. The Trollopes and fellow travelers "huddled themselves" into the vessel and "proceeded to carry on life there as though they were quite at home." The men made a beeline for the barroom, tossed down toddies and lit up stogies, while the women, denied that entertainment, "got themselves into rocking chairs in the salon and sat there listless and silent, but not more listless and silent then they usually are in the big drawing rooms of the big hotels."

Supper was served at 6:00 p.m. and, while dining, a fellow traveler informed Trollope of the rules of steamboat meals when a vessel was delayed: "Your first supper you pay for, because you eat that on your own account. What you consume after that comes of their doing, because they don't start; and if it's three meals a day for a week, it's their look out." It occurred to Trollope that to avoid the expense of free meals, "a captain would be very apt to sail in foul weather or in fair."

After dinner, Trollope took his stroll. Because the railroad depot was located on the west side of the Grand River opposite the village proper until 1870, Trollope never saw more of Grand Haven than the distant twinkling of kerosene lights across the river. What he actually viewed were the big sand dunes that stretched for miles along the lake, "great sand mountains, and sand valleys, on the surface of which were scattered the debris of dead trees, scattered logs white with age, and boughs half buried beneath the sand."

Having soon seen enough of the dunes to pillory the town in print forevermore, Trollope returned to the steamer's taproom, lit a cigar and leaned back. Ignoring his mother's censures of 30 years before, he planted his feet firmly on the bar and, with bright black eyes flashing behind his spectacles, in his deep bass voice entered a debate about the war. He found Maj. Gen. John Charles Fremont, the intrepid Rocky Mountains trailblazer and the first Republican candidate for president in 1856, the "hero of the hour." Fremont was then commander of the Western

This 1860s view of Grand Haven shows the railroad depot on the bank of the Grand River opposite the city.

Department, headquartered in St. Louis. One of the Michigan debaters told Trollope, "Why, sir; there are 50,000 men in these states who will follow Fremont, who would not stir a foot after any other man."

Unfortunately, popularity aside, Fremont proved an inept commander, spending huge sums to fortify his St. Louis headquarters while his ill- equipped soldiers repeatedly blundered into Confederate ambushes. Considered "one of the North's greatest military embarrassments," Fremont was relieved of all duties as a Union commander a few days after the discussion in the steamboat bar.

After the debate, Trollope turned in. During the night the steamer sailed and the British travelers found themselves at Milwaukee in time for breakfast, having, Trollope grumbled, "received no pecuniary advantage whatever from that law as to the steam-boat meals."

Following his nine-month tour of the northern states and Canada, Trollope returned to England in May 1862, where he rushed into print his ill-humored three-volume travel narrative.

The work sold well in Great Britain and he netted more money from it than he earned for *Barchester Towers*. Prior to his death in 1882, Trollope would write more than 90 novels, travel books and collections of essays. His literary reputation tumbled following his death, in part because he revealed in his autobiography that he treated literature as a trade and wrote by the clock. Some 20th-century critics have praised and resurrected his writings; none, however, to my knowledge, who hail from Detroit or Grand Haven.

The White Widow Among the Chippewa

Mary Cabay appreciated the tribe's many kindnesses following the death of her Chippewa husband in 1863. When the north wind blew across Saginaw Bay the white widow from Boston found particularly comforting the cord wood given by her husband's cousin, Peter Sagatoo. She repeatedly offered to pay him for the wood, but he always demurred. Sometimes he dropped off codfish he purchased in Bay City as he knew she relished that reminder of her old home.

Then one day her father-in-law, Cabay, and Sagatoo's father paid her a visit. Mary never forgot what Cabay told her: "It was a custom of his tribe that when a husband died, after one year the nearest relative would select another companion for the widow, and the man selected would take a load of wood to the woman, and if she burned the wood it was a sign she was willing to share his fireside, but if she refused to burn the wood they would select another man for her, and if she burned the wood and then refused to marry the man, she would be put to death."

"Now," he continued, his dark eyes boring into hers, "you have burned the wood Peter brought to you, what you going to do? Take Peter?"

The genesis of this matrimonial predicament came a decade before when 19-year-old Mary Henderson saw the light during a Methodist prayer meeting and determined to devote her life to missionary work in India. She began working her way through a nearby academy to prepare herself for the calling. Too many late night study vigils brought on a nervous condition, and a physician told her she must relinquish her studies. Furthermore, he told her, "With that trouble in your head you would not live three months in so hot a climate as India." She tempered her disappointment at not being able to "spend her life helping the

children in far off India" by immersing herself in pros-
elytizing Boston's Catholic children.

During a church meeting in 1860 she was introduced to Joseph Cabay, a well-educated Chippewa
from the Saginaw region. Over the next three years
while he attended Harvard University, they fell in love.
Cabay asked her to marry him and help him minister to

**Mary Sagatoo devoted herself to bettering her
adopted people's lives.**

Joseph Cabay brought his white wife back
to his Chippewa people, then died.

his people at the Saganing Mission on the shore of
Saginaw Bay, approximately 25 miles north of Bay
City. If her work was not to be in India, Mary ratio-
nalized, perhaps the Indians of Michigan would do.

Before they could tie the nuptial knot, Cabay
began complaining of severe chest pains. A renowned
lung doctor delivered the tragic diagnosis - "tuberculo-

sis had taken a firm hold on him, medicine would do him no good - he should return to Michigan as quickly as possible, that the breezes from the lakes might add a few days to his life."

Mary decided that as she had promised in health to become his wife she would not forsake him when he needed her care. Her father told her "she had taken leave of her senses to think of marrying a dying Indian" and refused to give her away. Nevertheless, on March 5, 1863, the minister pronounced them man and wife.

The newlyweds left for Michigan, sojourning at Niagara Falls for a few days where the chill damp air worsened Cabay's condition. By the time they reached Bay City he was bedridden. He had to be carried to a bed aboard a boat for the last leg of their journey. Arriving at Saganing, a Methodist mission established among the Chippewa by the Rev. George Bradley in 1846, they found that Cabay's family had not received the letter telling of their marriage. When informed of the fact by an interpreter, they all solemnly shook hands with Mary - some of the women kissed her.

At noon the next day, Chief Cabay blew a horn which summoned the Indians to his house. It was then that Joseph took his wife's hand and said: "Mary, my dear wife, I want you to make me a promise before I leave you. It is a hard one. Will you stay with my people, take my place among them, and try to do for them what I would have done if God had spared my life?"

She cried out, "Oh, Joseph, don't leave me, it so lonesome here!"

"Please," he implored, "make the promise and I shall die happier." He awaited her reply, his breath growing more labored.

Finally, she said, "Yes, I will do as you wish."

Then the chief approached the bedside to conduct the Chippewa adoption ceremony. Cabay placed Mary's hand over Joseph's and put his own atop hers, saying: "God is about taking my son Joseph to Himself. The love I have had for him I now give to you. You are hereafter a daughter to me in the same sense that he has been a son."

The chief then bestowed on Mary her new Chippewa name - *Wah Sash Kah Moqua,* meaning "there was darkness but your coming brings light."

Minutes later, Joseph breathed his last. Mary felt deeply the burden of her plight. She was alone in a wilderness far from the home and friends she had known all her life, among a people of strange beliefs who spoke but little English, and she understood not one sentence of Chippewa.

For many months after Joseph's death, she said her evening prayers at his grave then, laying her head on the sod beneath which he rested, she would "cry till I had no more tears to shed."

But she kept her promise to Joseph, staying among his people, gradually learning some of the language and Chippewa culture.

Some Indian customs troubled her. Her heart ached for "the poor squaws carrying heavy loads upon their backs, while the men would walk before them smoking their pipes." She learned that Chippewa creation myths told that the great Manabozho had created the first woman from the shoulder bone of man so women were thought to be the stronger and able to perform manual labor easier.

She also learned that, customarily, a Chippewa widow did not wash her face nor change her clothing for one full year. Then her wigwam, clothes and cooking utensils were burned. She was given new ones, along with a new husband. But no one bothered to inform Mary of the widow and wood custom until Cabay's startling ultimatum two years later.

Frightened, Mary asked why she had not been told of these customs before she burned the wood.

Cabay answered, "Because we want you to take Peter, he good man and likes you."

As soon as the Indians left her house, Mary stuffed her clothing in a trunk and hurried onto the next boat to Bay City. But when she arrived, Peter Sagatoo

Mary found happiness with Peter Sagatoo, her second Chippewa husband.

was waiting for her, having raced there on horseback. A long discussion with Mary ensued, during which, she recalled, "he seemed so sad I pitied him." They were married the next day.

The marriage proved a long and satisfying one, despite a later accident that blinded Peter in one eye. Mary devoted herself to bettering the lives of the Chippewa "children of the forest." She organized a school and became its teacher, spending most of her salary on clothes, food and medicine for the Indians. She traveled to Boston to raise funds for a new building to replace the primitive log cabin church. In 1874, the structure stood complete, financed in part by her own money.

After the dedication of the church, Joseph came down with typhoid fever. He survived, but the heartless medical bills brought on years of destitution and suffering. By the 1890s more than half of the approximately 400 Indians at Saganing had succumbed to the dread white man's diseases, tuberculosis, typhoid fever and small pox.

In an era when native Americans were considered less than human, Mary often endured the overt prejudice of nearby whites who more than once said in her presence, "If my sister or daughter married an Indian I would shoot her."

In 1897, Mary had published in Boston an account of her *Thirty-Three Years Among the Indians* to attempt to raise money for the couple's old age. Unfortunately, it sold poorly and is now a rare collector's item.

Of the more than 50 Methodist Indian missions founded in Michigan in the 19th-century, Saganing is one of but ten that survive. There, in the cemetery nearby the church she founded, sleep Mary and her two Chippewa husbands - graves unmarked but their selfless dedication remembered.

A Michigan Civil War Florence Nightingale

The sad wreckage of war littered the floor of the big Fredericksburg, Virginia church. Pews removed, the makeshift hospital sheltered some two hundred of the shattered boys in blue who flowed in May 1864, from the butchery of the Wilderness and Spotsylvania.

A Michigan heroine stepped gingerly through the writhing rug of tattered, mud and blood soaked uniforms, of jagged undressed wounds and the stumps of amputated limbs. Steeling herself against the sights and stench of death, Julia Wheelock worked feverishly, binding wounds, ladling chicken broth, here answering a croak for water, there for a pillow to soften the ache of the hard wooden floor.

It was then that she heard a beautiful clear tenor singing an old joyful hymn. She traced the tune to a youth, horribly wounded in both arms, who had been propped against the wall. Tears trickled down Julia's face as she listened to that sweet voice rise above the moans and groans of the rest.

That was but one of the many indelible memories that marked her three years as an angel of mercy to the Michigan soldiers who suffered in our nation's terrible Civil War.

Born in Avon, Ohio, in 1833, Julia joined two brothers who had established farms near Ionia, Michigan, after the death of her parents. Intelligent and determined to advance, she attended Kalamazoo College from 1858-1860. She then secured a job as a teacher in a rural school near her brothers' farms.

She was busy with student recitations on the afternoon of September 10, 1862, when a tearful neighbor girl burst in with news that Julia's brother Orville, a sergeant in Company K, 8th Michigan Infantry, had been badly wounded in the Battle of Chantilly, Virginia. His arm had been amputated.

Knowing the abysmal medical facilities of the Civil War era, relatives commonly rushed to the front to locate and arrange for better care of wounded loved ones. Julia, Orville's wife Anna, and her sister, Mrs. Peck, whose husband had also been wounded, traveled by rail and boat to reach Washington three days later.

Persistent appeals to the military bureaucracy by Julia finally yielded passes to proceed to Alexandria. Then came a desperate search through the city's 15 military hospitals, resulting only in the tragic discovery that Wheelock was already dead and buried. Months later, Julia learned the extent of Orville's suffering from a comrade who had stayed with his wounded friend. He laid for five days on the battlefield before a surgeon sawed off his arm and loaded him into an ambulance for the jarring 20 mile ride to Alexandria. Wheelock died three days later.

Second Michigan Infantry Chaplain Frank W. May from Kalamazoo consoled the heart-broken women. Before returning home Julia and Anna stopped at the office of the Michigan Soldiers Relief Association to enlist help in applying for a widow's pension for Anna.

That organization had been created to provide liaison between Michigan servicemen and their families, to distribute food, clothing and other supplies sent from Michigan and, in general, to offer the types of services that would be supplied by the Red Cross after its founding by Clara Barton in 1881.

Impressed with the good being done by the organization, Julia saw a way that she might serve the cause for which her brother had given his life. She joined Elmira Brainard of Lapeer as the second "lady agent" of the association. They received no pay, merely a $5 per week room and board allowance, yet soon expanded their role to that of sorely needed nurses.

Julia spent long days trudging through the 20 Washington schools, churches and mansions (some containing 1,500 patients) that had been converted to military hospitals. She sought out Michigan boys, noted their wants, helped them compose letters, soothed fevered brows and held the hands of the dying. She dispensed shirts, socks, towels, handkerchiefs and pillows. She spooned out helpings of stewed tomatoes and raspberry sauce, mugs of chicken broth and hot tea. She meted out fresh bread spread with applebutter, cheese, pickles, lemon slices and crisp Michigan apples. She frequently stayed up until midnight cooking huge cauldrons of chicken soup and twenty or more

Kalamazoo College-educated Julia Wheelock witnessed the horrors of Civil War hospitals.

pies. But she always reserved a few minutes before falling exhausted into bed to record her day's activities in the big journals she kept for three years. They served as the basis of her 1870 book *The Boys in White.*

Julia found the most appalling conditions about a mile and a half from the city at a wretched convalescent camp the soldiers called "Camp Misery." There, ten to fifteen thousand soldiers sick with fever, pneumonia, chronic diarrhea, and other diseases that would ultimately kill more men than battle wounds, camped out in tents on the damp ground, often without blankets or overcoats. Their rations consisted of rock-hard crackers and salt pork. With little or no firewood, they frequently gulped down the pork raw.

A contingent of 200 Michigan troopers had been allotted a campsite on a hillside. When it rained the water rushed through like a river. To keep their clothing dry they stood upright all night. In cold weather, without blankets they walked around beating their arms all night to keep from freezing to death.

Assisted by Chaplain May's wife, Julia made Camp Misery a special project. They visited often, laden with pies and stewed fruit, quilts and clothing. They also grew adept at circumventing regulations, spiriting away the sickest of the men to hospitals where they stood at least a chance of survival.

In December 1862, James A. B. Stone, president of Kalamazoo College, visited his former student. He accompanied her on hospital rounds so he could tell the folks back in Kalamazoo of her splendid work. A year later, Liberty Holden, one of her professors at the college, also called upon her. Impressed by the importance of her mission, he said: "We didn't know what we were preparing you for, when you were with us in Kalamazoo. We never dreamed that you would so soon engage in work like this."

Julia recorded in her book page after page of

poignant stories that eclipse glorious cavalry charges and dashing deeds to capture the true measure of war. She wrote of the four boys from the same Michigan family that perished in three months time - of the Michigan man who suffered an excruciating death because of cayenne pepper-laced bandages contributed by a southern sympathizer - of the desperate pleas for food and blankets she could not satisfy - of fanning from the faces of dying soldiers the flies that "buzzed and swarmed like bees."

In 1864, when Grant's and Lee's armies grappled in Virginia and Fredericksburg groaned with 10,000 or more of the bloody aftermath, Julia recorded her most horrifying experiences. She saw great stacks of amputated limbs at field hospitals and practically every available church, store or school crowded with the maimed. She grieved for the Michigan soldiers she knelt over who she thought had no chance of survival - Ann Arbor's Sgt. William Clark of the 8th Michigan with a minie ball lodged in the back of his mouth, Capt. James Donahue of Flint and Lt. John C. Joss of Constantine, both with legs amputated at the thigh. Ultimately the Civil War claimed the lives of more than 500,000 Union and Confederate soldiers through combat and disease. Miraculously, Clark, Donahue and Joss survived their terrible wounds to appear in many a hometown Memorial Day parade.

Worn-out by her long hours of devotion, Julia succumbed to fever in July 1864. Following a four week convalescence she toured Michigan, raising funds for the boys fighting not to "exchange their suit of blue for a robe of white." She ended her war service in June, 1865. Eight years later she married Porter Freeman, moved to Middleville, then Marshall and raised two sons. In 1890, ten years before her death, a special act of Congress awarded Julia a $12 per month military pension for her service during the "War of the Rebellion."

The Shooting Of Sheriff Orcutt

Kalamazoo County Sheriff Benjamin F. Orcutt, a veteran of two wars, knew well how to "sleep with one eye open." He lay particularly alert the night of December 2, 1867, because among the inmates lodged in the old ramshackle jail built in 1845 just south of the courthouse were a pair of desperate burglars, members of a Chicago gang. About three in the morning, a slight noise aroused Orcutt from his uneasy slumber. Springing from bed, he grabbed his revolver and dashed out the door of his residence attached to the rear of the jail. Racing around the building, he spied two men beneath one of the jail windows. The pair took flight.

Orcutt yelled "halt" and gave chase, firing as he ran. The fugitives darted across Michigan Avenue then split up. One continued north and the other holed up behind a big oak tree in an alley between Rose and Burdick streets. As the sheriff approached, three shots rang out. Orcutt went down, calling for help.

The commotion awoke tenants in a nearby boarding house who scrambled to assist the sheriff. Regaining his feet, he staggering back toward the jail. Orcutt's wife Emily met him at the gate, but because he said nothing of his wound she thought his heavy breathing the result of his running. As a crowd collected, Orcutt insisted on returning to the corner of the jail where he had surprised the pair to ascertain if any of the prisoners had escaped. None had, and only when he was satisfied that the crowd of citizens would prevent any further escape attempts did he enter his house. Recalling the shots she had heard, Emily ask him if he thought he had killed anyone. "No," he replied, "but I think he has killed me."

She summoned physicians who soon diagnosed but faint hope for his survival. A bullet had entered near

102

his right collar bone and exited near the left shoulder blade, grazing a major artery, a condition that the medical technology of that time was powerless to remedy. Orcutt lingered until the evening of December 12, when he quietly passed away.

Born in Roxbury, near Vermont's Green Mountains, in 1815, Orcutt had immigrated to Detroit at the age of 19. A few months later he continued west to Chicago where he resided for a year. He spent the following year in the newly-platted community of Allegan before settling in Kalamazoo in 1836. Five years later, he was elected the town's constable and

Sheriff Benjamin Orcutt served as lieutenant colonel of the 25th Michigan Infantry during the Civil War.

later served as a deputy U.S. marshal. Following the outbreak of the Mexican War, in 1847 Orcutt was one of the hundred Kalamazoo men who volunteered for the regiment organized by Capt. Frederick Curtenius. The unit reached Mexico in January 1848, where First Sergeant Orcutt saw action against guerrillas.

Orcutt won election as Kalamazoo County sheriff in 1854 and 1858. In 1862 he enlisted in the 25th Michigan Infantry, serving as lieutenant colonel under Col. Orlando Wilcox throughout the war. The regiment distinguished itself, in particular, at the Battle of Tebb's Bend, Kentucky, and during the Atlanta Campaign. Orcutt returned to Kalamazoo in 1865 and the following year was again elected sheriff.

In the light of day following Orcutt's shooting, citizens discovered a jack screw, tarred rope and a kit of burglar tools near the oak tree in the alley. Blood spots nearby indicated the sheriff had probably wounded one of the criminals.

Amid talk of lynching some of the prisoners in the county jail by way of retaliation, a mass meeting of Kalamazooans assembled and elected a committee to coordinate efforts to apprehend the villains. Based on contemporary newspaper articles and statements by Emily Orcutt, Samuel Durant in his monumental 1880 *History of Kalamazoo County,* noted that: "Telegrams were sent in all directions, and every means was employed to sift the matter to the bottom, but the real criminals were never discovered."

However, a more detailed account of the murder which appeared 12 years later in the voluminous *Portrait and Biographical Record of Kalamazoo, Van Buren and Allegan Counties* offers a more satisfying outcome to the story.

It seems that Kalamazoo officials hired private detectives from Chicago who, several months after the shooting, captured one of the fugitives, Hugh Darraugh. Tried and sentenced to six years in the

Jackson Penitentary as an accomplice, Darraugh died in prison. Eighteen months after the crime, the famous detective agency founded by Alan Pinkerton under the motto "we never sleep" tracked the other murderer, Stephen Boyle, to New York City.

One hundred and thirty years after the murder, a "confidential" $500 reward circular sent by Orcutt's successor, Sheriff John H. Wells, to Chicago Chief of Police Jacob Rehm surfaced in a rare book dealer's catalog. The poster sheds some final intriguing light on the man who killed Kalamazoo's popular sheriff, revealing what he looked like:

> *Stephen Boyle, alias Guss Shaw, alias Charles Shaw, is 5 feet, 6-3/4 inches high, light complexion, light and thin hair, dark blue eyes, slim built, 25 years old; weight about 125 lbs; small foot, wears a No. 5 boot; walks very straight; has the asthma very bad; will probably wear a sandy moustache to hide the upper teeth which are very much decayed; lower teeth good and even; the upper lip is large and homely.*

Setting aside the fact that a homely upper lip would be difficult to distinguish camouflaged behind a moustache ample enough to hide bad teeth, this rare scrap of ephemera, most probably a unique document, survived the ravages of time to put a face, albeit it one only a mother could love, on the desperado who had such a doleful effect on Kalamazoo's history. The circular also captured Boyle's life style for posterity:

> *He is very dressy and proud, usually wears a high silk hat. Stephen Boyle is well known in New York City as a pickpocket, burglar and sneak thief; has traveled in almost every state, and is well known by all the thieves as Stephe the Stage Busser*

(underworld slang for a thief) of New York; is an escaped convict from Sing Sing, N.Y. and Joliet, Ill.; will probably stop at some private boarding house; will be found with Eastern thieves.

The Pinkertons shadowed Boyle for three months in New York before teaming up with the local police to nab him red-handed during a burglary. Sheriff Wells attempted to extradite Boyle, but because of his long criminal record in New York, authorities there quickly sentenced the "busser" to 40 years in Sing Sing, a place where he was no stranger.

Sheriff Orcutt's funeral was "very solemn and imposing, a vast concourse of people turning out to pay respect." Officals draped the court house in black. Following his burial in Mountain Home Cemetery, Kalamazoo citizens raised $600 to erect a suitable marble monument over his grave.

The sheriff's funeral expenses came from county coffers. But that is where government generosity ended. In an era when death benefits or pensions were scarcely heard of, tight-fisted county commissioners voted against implementing a state legislative act which authorized the county to levy a tax of $2,000 for the maintenance and education of Orcutt's three young sons.

In 1882, Kalamazoo Civil War veterans named their Grand Army of the Republic post in Orcutt's honor. It continued to perpetuate his memory until its disbandment in 1943. And so ends the story of Benjamin Orcutt, who according to research by former Kalamazoo County Clerk Jim Youngs, was Michigan's first sheriff to be killed in the line of duty.

"Curfew Must Not Ring Tonight"

As the chalk clicked rhythmically across the slate, sixteen-year-old Rose Hartwick seemed intent on her homework. Earlier that day the schoolmaster berated her for inattention and her mother scolded not to fritter away time dreaming about the poetry that was her passion. She had solemnly promised to obey, then sat down to study by the light of the fireplace. But even as she clutched the dog-eared arithmetic text, thoughts returned to the story that had haunted her since reading it the day before in a popular magazine. Over and over she mulled the phrase, "Curfew must not ring tonight."

Then she began to write, lost in the 17th century English Civil War that pitted merciless Oliver Cromwell's Puritans against the Cavaliers. Verse after verse flowed down the hand slate, front and back. Only after finishing the poem did her mind spring back to her own time - April 5, 1867, in the little community of Litchfield in northwest Hillsdale County.

By then it was bedtime and her real lessons lay untouched. Appalled, the sensitive teenager tearfully gushed: "Oh! mother dear, I can hardly believe it, but I could not help it. I didn't intend to deceive you. I did just what I promised you I would not do. I sat down with the full intention of writing nothing but my lessons, and before I knew it, these verses came and I had to write them. Just let me read them to you, then I will wash them off my slate, forget them and do my lessons." The wise mother stayed her chide and listened:

"England's sun was slowly setting o'er the hilltops far away,

Filling all the land with beauty at the close of one sad day;

And its last rays kissed the forehead of a man and maiden fair,...

"Sexton," Bessie's white lips faltered, pointing to the prison old,

With its walls so tall and gloomy, moss-grown walls dark, damp and cold, —

"I've a lover in that prison, doomed this very night to die

At the ringing of the curfew; and no earthly help is nigh.

Cromwell will not come till sunset;" and her lips grew strangely white,

As she spoke in husky whispers, "Curfew must not ring to-night."

An 1887 edition of Rose Hartwick Thorpe's famous poem included an illustration of the heroine's jump for the clapper.

As Rose read on, her mother, too, felt transport-ed across the Atlantic to a place and time she had never been. She heard Bessie's betrothed falsely accused of spying and quickly sentenced to death. She listened to

Bessie desperately attempt to avert the execution until Cromwell might intercede by begging the sexton to delay the nightly curfew bell. But the old man had insisted on doing his duty. Rushing unseen to the top of the ancient belfry, Bessie leaped up and clung to the big bell's clapper as the deaf sexton tolled the muffled curfew. When:

> *O'er the distant hills comes Cromwell. Bessie sees him; and her brow,*
> *Lately white with sickening horror, has no anxious traces now.*
> *At his feet she tells her story, shows her hands all bruised and torn;*
> *And her sweet young face, still haggard, with the anguish it had worn,*
> *Touched his heart with sudden pity, lit his eyes with misty light.*
> *"Go! your lover lives," cried Cromwell. "Curfew shall not ring to-night!"*

Finished, Rose reached to wipe the slate clean when her mother cried out: "Wait awhile, child, let them stay on your slate until morning. Never mind your lessons. I think I would like you to write those verses on paper tomorrow so that we may keep them."

And thus was spared what would become one of the best-loved poems of the 19th-century. Those verses, which generations of children in one-room country schoolhouse and big city academies memorized and recited before audiences of proud parents, would find their way into countless anthologies and be translated into scores of tongues. And its Michigan author reaped enduring fame, but not a cent of profit.

Born in Mishawaka, Indiana, in 1850, one of five children of pioneer farm folk, Rose immigrated with her family to Kansas ten years later. A relentless drought on the plains spelled disaster for the western venture and the Hartwicks retreated to Litchfield where relatives offered succor. The family breadwinner eked out a living as a tailor, but poverty prevented the purchase of the books which Rose craved even as a child.

Her mother marked early Rose's poetic flair when she overheard her reciting original verses to dolls. At the age of 11 she began contributing poems about local happenings to the Litchfield High School paper. Rose's poetic horizons broadened when she received a volume of Lord Byron's poems for her 15th birthday. She memorized nearly every line of that great romantic poet's work.

A neighboring physician kindly loaned copies of *Peterson's Magazine* to the dreamy-eyed teenager who hungered for any and all reading matter. In the September 1865 issue she encountered the anonymous article, "Love and Loyalty," that so gripped her imagination and led to the creation of "Curfew Must Not Ring To-Night."

Fulfilling her mother's request, she copied the poem into a little leather-bound blank book that held other of her juvenile effusions. And there it lay, known only to family members, for three years. In the meantime, she had submitted a poem to the Detroit *Commercial Advertiser*. In an era when poetry occupied a far more important place in America's everyday life than now, newspapers frequently included amateur verse. To Rose's glee, the editor published the piece and wrote her that while he could not afford to pay, in return for additional verses he would mail a gratis subscription to the paper, a $1.50 per year value.

Proud that readers outside of Litchfield valued her work, Rose dutifully sent the Detroit skinflint a poem each week. But in 1870 she caught typhoid fever. Too sick to write her weekly piece, she forwarded instead the curfew poem. The editor published it in Rose's usual "poetry corner." Its dramatic appeal and joyous ending struck sentimental Victorian fancy in a

Rose Hartwick at the age of 16.

way few other poems had. At a time when newspaper writings were rarely copyrighted, other papers, magazines and journals brazenly reprinted the piece. As paper after paper copied the ballad, students began reciting it, as well as teachers, preachers, professional elocutionists and platform orators on both sides of the Atlantic. It became a personal favorite of Queen Victoria, herself.

Rose, who in 1871 had married Litchfield carriage maker Edmund C. Thorpe and traded the visionary quest of the poet for the practical reality of raising a brood of youngsters, remained unaware of her literary child's amazing success. In 1879, A.A. Hopkins highlighted the poem with a biography of Rose in a compilation of newspaper poetry, *Waifs, and Their Authors.* "Curfew" also found its way into dozens of the then-popular recitation manuals.

But bad luck in the form of illness and a faltering business dogged the Thorpes. They moved to Chicago in 1881, where Rose supplemented their precarious existence with the few dollars she earned from writing for religious and juvenile publications. Then came a ray of hope. Lee & Shepard, a prominent Boston publisher, wrote Rose seeking to publish "Curfew" in an elaborate illustrated edition. Naively relying on the firm's fairness, she gave permission and even supplied an additional final verse. The unscrupulous publisher promptly copyrighted the entire poem in its name, and Rose never received a nickle of royalties for the best seller.

The Thorpes moved to Grand Rapids in 1883. That year Hillsdale College awarded Rose an honorary Master of Arts for her poem. But that degree did little to enhance her financial plight. Rose continued to write hundreds of fugitive pieces and a score of mawkish books. None of those long-forgotten celebrations of "mother, home and heaven" proved very successful.

When Edward contracted tuberculosis, the family moved to the more salubrious climate of San Antonio, Texas. Four years later they relocated to San Diego, California, where Rose remained until her death in 1939.

In 1935, proud Litchfield residents erected a monument to Rose. On a foundation of choice fieldstones from nearby farms stands the old village bell that for generations tolled tidings of funerals, weddings and fire alarms, an ironic memorial to a famous poem about a bell that did not ring.

Of Goats, Gillens &
Green Gold!

It was an 1873 Saturday night in a snow-muf-fled lumber camp far up Alpena County's Thunder Bay River. A half hundred recruits of the "Cant Hook Brigade" - brawny Swedes, auburn Celts, old woods-men from Maine and a sprinkling of French "Canucks" - had moiled among the "green gold," as the towering white pine were known, from dawn to dusk through the bitter cold of the previous six days. Now, having bolt-ed a huge supper, it was time for a little fun.

The "caboose," an open fireplace laid on a stone and sand foundation in the center of the rough log camp house, blazed cheerily, casting a ruddy glow on the long row of bunks, the network of wire clothes-drying racks and the shanty boys clad in red sus-penders, Mackinaw shirts and wool socks rolled over the tops of big leather boots. The smoke from numer-ous pipes mingled with that of the poorly vented fire as the program began with a ballad a cappella:

"Come all you jolly lumbermen,
Wherever you may be
I pray you pay attention
And listen unto me
'Tis of some jolly lumbermen
Who did agree to go
And spend the winter pleasantly
In Michigan - I - O.

Then came clog dancing, sentimental poetry recitations and stories of legendary Alpena barroom brawlers. The talk of fights spurred some of the boys to debate the relative merits of the U.S. and Canadian governments. One old jack nearly brought the entire camp to fisticuffs when he bellowed, "I'd rather be hanged in Michigan then die a natural death in

Canada!" But the boys were just marking time for the highlight of the evening - the initiation ceremony of the "goat."

Charley, a handsome, muscular 20-year-old, had joined the crew the week before. He had left his father's farm in western Ontario, like many another young Canadian of the era, to seek his fortune in the booming Michigan tall timber trade, where men earned $30 - $40 a month and board for their dangerous labors. Well-dressed and educated, Charley did not fit the mold of the typical shanty boy. Worse yet, he "talked too much and ranked so high in his own estimation, backed up by his superior knowledge and learning, that he made the rest of the crew look cheap by comparison." It had not taken the boys long to decide who

Michigan shanty boys worked from dawn to dusk making "light in the swamp."

would be the goat for the upcoming Saturday night.

After the singing and storytelling, someone proposed a game of "Twin Brothers." Two of the jacks lay face down on the floor beneath a blanket on which was placed a small stick. The rest of the crew marched in a circle around the men on the floor. Periodically one would grab the stick, tap one of the twins, quickly drop the stick and keep marching. The twin tapped would pop his head out of the blanket and attempt to name who hit him. If he was right, the guilty player exchanged places with him.

Charley joined in, ventured to strike one of the twins a light blow and soon found himself under the blanket. Then his fellow twin reached out his strong right arm, made a motion with his hand and someone slipped him a stout hickory stick. He cracked Charley hard on the ribs. The Canadian popped-up with "blood in his eye," quickly guessed the wrong man, then warned if he was hit again like that there would be the devil to pay. Resuming his place under the blanket, he received a sharp whack to his behind. Jumping to his feet as if he'd been "stung by a hornet," Charley was hopping mad. He threatened to "punch the head off the whelp that hit him that cowardly blow, and begged him to come forward and be murdered." When the jacks merely looked around in innocent surprise, he offered to "lick any man in the camp." After Charley stormed around the room "with the clouds of war dancing polkas across his brow" for a while, the crew managed to calm him by assuring it had all been an innocent mistake. Sheepishly, Charley apologized for having made a row over such a trivial matter.

Round two of the goat's initiation began when one of the boys offered to "pull sticks" with any man in camp. In pulling sticks two men sat on the floor, facing each other with the soles of their feet touching. Each grabbed a two foot long stick and upon command, pulled until the lower part of the weaker contestant's

One of the largest loads of white pine ever drawn by one team, 30,068 board-feet, came from the woods near Oscoda in the 1880s.

body was drawn two or three feet into the air.

Gardner Nicholson, the strongest man in camp, took the floor first and quickly defeated four or five challengers. Then a jack hollered from the back of the crowd that he would "bet a pack of chewing tobacco that Charley could pull Nicholson through his collar!" Flattered, Charley took the stick with the strong man. Nicholson closed his eyes, gave a grunt as he strained back and Charley slowly rose four feet in the air. One of the crew slid a big dish pan filled with ice cold water beneath Charley. Nicholson's hands "somehow slipped," and the Canadian dropped like a rock. Water jetted high, flooding the floor and dousing the fire in the caboose. Shocked by the icy bath, Charley shot to his feet. Then his face grew "pale with rage, his eyes danced in his head like balls of fire!" "Let the dastardly, contemptible low-down skunk who played that trick identify himself so I can dry up the floor with his scurvy carcass," he roared! Again, the boys had no idea who might have done the deed.

Later, when the goat had cooled down, the conspirators agreed that Saturday night had been "more fun than a barrel of monkeys." As for Charley, he became one of the camp's more humble souls.

James Collins preserved the story of Charley's evolution from goat to jack in his 1914 pamphlet, *Life in a Lumber Camp.* Born in Ontario in 1851, Collins immigrated with his parents to Alpena as a child. Prior to 1873 he spent several seasons in nearby lumber camps before earning a law degree and editing several Alpena newspapers. Because of his intimate knowledge of Charley's thoughts and feelings, he likely was describing his own experiences as a goat.

In any event, Collins' colorful anecdotes in lumberjack lingo offer a crystal clear glimpse of shanty boy life when pine was king in Michigan.

Though romanticized in novels, verse and song,

in an era when most Americans earned their livelihood through "the sweat of their brow," toil in the tall timber proved particularly brutal. The chore-boy, a jack-of-all-trades assistant to the foreman, aroused the camp with the clank of a cow bell and the "dismal yell," "Turn-Out!" at 4 a.m. First up were the teamsters and log loaders.

Each night the men hung their wet clothing and socks on a system of racks and hooks that ringed the caboose. Collins noted: "The aroma that issued from those steaming socks filled the camp with a fragrance which was different from that of new mowed hay, or attar of roses." The law of the lumber camp decreed that the men first out in the morning were the most warmly dressed for the day. Accordingly, they freely helped themselves to the newest and best grade of socks. The owner of comfortable all-wool socks "soon learned to dry them by hand in the evening, and then hide them under his pillow."

Except for Sunday or an occasional "Gillen," a much-welcomed day too stormy to work in the woods, the rest of the crew climbed out of their cedar branch-mattressed bunks at 5:00 a.m., quickly dressed in the cold and headed to the cook camp for a hurried breakfast. The choppers and sawyers who felled the timber and crosscut it into 16-foot lengths usually found themselves out in the woods in sub-zero weather shuffling around bonfires until it was light enough to work.

The lumber work force included numerous gangs who practiced specialized tasks. Road makers constructed and kept the roads in repair. Swampers cut the trails for skidders who dragged logs with oxen to the skidways and decked them in piles. Using cant hooks, loaders positioned logs on big bob sleighs to be hauled by horses managed by teamsters to the river landing. There, landing men unloaded and banked them into mountain-high stacks. During the spring log drive, river men or "river hogs" rode the logs downstream, balancing themselves with long handled peaveys, retrieving beached logs and breaking up dangerous log jams. A floating cookhouse called a wannigan followed the drive.

The system usually worked well except when someone trespassed on another's well-defined area of authority. Teamsters, for example, determined how many logs a sleigh load held based on knowledge of their horses' capacity. When a "boss-loader" attempted to overload there was apt to be a fist fight. Collins wrote: "A boss-loader in a lumber camp was never popular with the teamsters. If he was an agreeable sort of a fellow, he wouldn't be a boss-loader."

Most of the crew knocked off work at dusk, making their way back to camp by 6:00 p.m. But the teamsters and landing men continued until the last load reached the river landing, returning to camp for "cold beans" sometimes four hours later. At camp the other shanty boys washed up in basins and anxiously awaited the cookee's shout, "TAKE "ER -R!" Whereupon they rushed for the cook camp and wolfed down prodigious meals. Before turning in about 10 p.m., the men lounged in the bunk house or sharpened and repaired their equipment. The next morning brought "the same thing over again."

Yet, despite the back-breaking labor and misery, Collins and many another old shanty boy lamented the passing of the days when pine was king, a glorious era when "the man who could not fall timber without breaking it on a stump or across a sharp knoll, build a skidway, or skid 300 logs with an ox team and one swamper in a day, drive a horse-team, carry lunch, flip a cant hook, or ride a log over Trowbridge's dam when the water was at high tide in the spring time, without wetting his feet, had no standing in Alpena's best society."

When A "Sucker" Pulled The Plug Of Crystal Lake

Archibald Jones stroked his long, white beard in satisfaction that late September morning in 1873 as a sweating shoveler shivered the final sliver of sand blocking the outlet of Crystal Lake. Jones and the many local backers of the Betsie River Improvement Company had sunk plenty of capital and months of hard labor into the project intended to open the region to Lake Michigan shipping. Now, as the first water trickled into the mile-long artificial channel painstakingly scooped to the Betsie River, more than one of those Benzie County speculators rubbed his palms in anticipation of imminent financial gain.

Within minutes the current quickened, rapidly eating away the sugar-soft sand. An hour later the flow had became an uncontrollable torrent. By noon Benzonia residents, five miles distant, distinctly heard the Niagara-like roar of the vast volume of white water churning the channel. Even as carriage loads from Benzonia and Frankfort flocked to the spectacle, no one yet suspected that something in the scheme had gone terribly awry.

Jones, an enterprising entrepreneur from Illinois, like many another "Sucker State" resident had heeded the call of Michigan's pristine north country in the early 1870s. Installing his family in a rambling mansion built by a Benzonia physician, the former orchard keeper sized up the surroundings for a fruitful venture. By 1873 he had devised a plan to link Crystal Lake with the Betsie River via canal so that medium-sized vessels could steam up from Frankfort Harbor on Lake Michigan. Vast forests of pine and hardwoods extended for miles from the banks of undeveloped Crystal Lake, a frigid, deep, spring-fed, three-by-eight-mile oval of blue beauty, so named because of the clarity of its waters. All that was needed to capitalize on

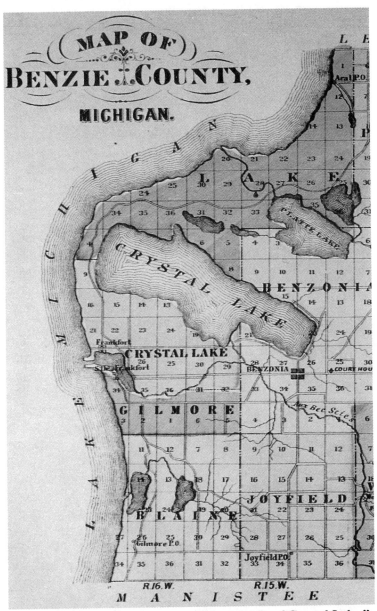

This 1884 map shows the scene of "the tragedy of Crystal Lake."

this wealth of timber was a means of transporting logs and tanbark to Frankfort docks and cord wood to the thriving charcoal-fired iron furnaces at South Frankfort.

An able promoter, the patriarchal-appearing Jones soon convinced numerous locals to subscribe to the company he organized to prosecute the venture. The Betsie River Improvement Company, with Jones as president, purchased land on Crystal Lake and set to work straightening and deepening the foot-deep outlet creek that meandering lazily through the lowlands to the Betsie River, a mile distant. The company also contracted for construction of a specially designed steamboat.

The scheme seemed so straightforward and simple that no one apparently took the precaution of consulting a reliable engineer as to its feasibility. Therein lurked a problem. Rather than being a few feet above the level of Lake Michigan, as was suspected, the surface of Crystal Lake lapped a good 30-feet higher.

Throughout the summer, Jones supervised the construction crew which gouged out the new outlet canal using horse drawn scrapers and shovels. Meanwhile, John Torrence, a master ship builder from Manistee, proceeded to lay the keel of the steamer on the bank of the Betsie River below Benzonia.

Things progressed so well that Jones hatched an even more grandiose scheme - why not expand the project to embrace Platte Lake to the north? He planned to dig a canal connecting Crystal and Platte lakes via a series of small lakes between and dam up the existing outlet of Platte Lake, thereby sending the entire Platte River system coursing through Crystal Lake, down the Betsie River and on to Frankfort's waiting lumber mills.

For some reason Jones decided to check the feasibility of this more ambitious undertaking by surveying the course. Surveyor John Barley set out from

Platte Lake with a compass and level. He had not gotten far before he realized he was heading uphill. Jones reluctantly dropped that portion of the master plan when Bailey explained that a canal cut between the lakes would only drain Crystal into Platte. Stifling any errant thoughts that there might be something equally amiss with tapping the other end of Crystal Lake, Jones pushed the excavation crew to complete its task.

On that fateful Saturday morning when they pulled the plug of Crystal Lake, things still seemed to be going as expected. Jones had hoped that the unleashed current would dredge its own channel through any remaining sand bars or other obstacles in the route to Frankfort. That it certainly did, along the newly dug outlet. But when the wall of water hit the bed of the Betsie River, it shot straight across it, "filling the lowlands on both sides and carrying hundreds of stranded saw logs away back in the swamp to the very edge of the highland bluffs." The torrent soon flooded the entire river valley, destroying roads and crops, and sweeping the bloated bodies of drowned cattle and swine downstream.

A stranger named Peacock who attempted to cross the Betsie at the long established ford drowned in the fierce current - his body lodged in a fallen tree top far downstream. The Rev. Adoniram Joy, a local Baptist preacher, nearly met a similar fate. He managed to struggle to shore, but his horse and buckboard were swept away.

The Sunday afternoon following "the letting of the blood," the *Onward*, a small steamship loaded with a dozen brave souls, cast off from her dock at Frankfort for "a voyage of adventure and discovery" up the river. By careful navigation her captain nosed the craft up the outlet into Crystal Lake. Tooting her whistle repeatedly to celebrate the inauguration of steamboat traffic on the lake, the vessel toured its circumference, stopping periodically to pick up cheering spectators. The return trip down the fierce current proved a perilous undertaking and, once safely docked in Frankfort, an experience which all aboard delighted in retelling many years later.

Jones embraced the *Onward's* voyage as proof of the practicality of his project, and there was great rejoicing among fellow stockholders. Alas, the jubilation proved short lived. The lake continued to bleed its blue waters until after two weeks the outlet steam reverted to its former narrow dribble. As the water level dropped and the lake shrank, a wide beach of bleaching sand and rock developed, an extensive sand bar formed a peninsula that ran far out into the lake and the once beautiful Crystal Lake became little more than a "desolate looking mill pond."

The investors' high hopes plummeted about as fast as the lake level. But Jones rallied his glum partners with the prospect of the profits still to be salvaged by transporting forest products from Benzonia to Frankfort's wharfs via the steamer under construction. The 12-foot-wide and 40-foot-long flat-bottomed river boat was launched early the following summer. Her stack belched black and her paddle wheel lashed white water as a crowd of Benzonians cheered her off on the maiden voyage.

But that trip down the river also proved "a most grievous disappointment." The Betsie simply had not enough depth to float a craft much larger than a canoe. For much of the distance the boat inched stern first, beating the sandy bottom with her wheel to dredge out a channel. Christened the *Mud Hen* by locals, the vessel never even attempted the return voyage. She operated as a tugboat in Frankfort for a time and later became a serviceable riverboat on the upper Mississippi River. And thus were dashed the last hopes of the Betsie River Improvement Company.

Worse yet, the builder of the *Mud Hen* sued for

non-payment. Jones mounted a noble defense in court, claiming the vessel was faultily constructed. But when pressed by the plaintiff's attorney as to the real reason why the boat would not navigate the Betsie, he admitted, "it was because the bottom of the river is too close to the top of the water."

That statement clinched the case for the plaintiff who took title to property the company had purchased. Jones soon returned to his Illinois home, never more to meddle with natural Michigan.

Eventually Crystal Lake regained some of its size when citizens constructed a dam at the outlet. In 1880, developers platted at the foot of the lake where a splendid wide beach now lay, the Crystal Lake and Beulah View Resort, later shortened to Beulah.

Nine years later, the Frankfort and Southern Railroad laid tracks along six miles of the beach where previously the lake lay five feet deep. The railroad and promotion of Crystal Lake's dazzling beaches helped the region develop into one of the state's most spectacular resorts. In 1916, the Betsie County Courthouse moved from Honor to Beulah.

Ultimately, Jones' blunder became Beulah's blessing.

The Benzie County Court House moved to this former amusement center known as the "Grand" in Beulah in 1916.

The Day Michigan
Burned Its Thumb

The hot wind blustered strong from the southwest as a big blood-red ball rose in the east on September 5, 1881. Eyes smarting from the acrid haze of white smoke, Ira Humphrey saddled his horse. Wild fires had raged in the "Thumb" for weeks and with the gusty wind Humphrey's wife Martha pleaded with him to stay home that day. But the postman prided himself on his record of always getting the mail through on time to the hamlets and crossroad outposts scattered throughout southwest Sanilac County. Kissing his wife goodbye, the 50-year-old swung easily into the saddle and cantered to Marlette.

As he filled his saddlebags with the day's mail, townspeople warned of the fierce forest fire roaring to the west. Humphrey boasted, "My horse can outrun any fire that ever burned," and then he rode north - straight into the jaws of fiery hell.

It had been an exceptionally dry summer. Not a drop of rain had spattered the dusty roads in two months. The merciless sun baked and cracked the soil and the sere underbrush rasped in the breeze. Old timers likened the drought to the parched summer and fall of 1871, when an October forest fire burned a swath across the state from the shore of Lake Michigan to Lake Huron, devastating two and a half million acres and numerous towns.

Thousands of acres of bone-dry dead trees stood as a reminder of that catastrophe. The big pines that had escaped the fire of 1871 had soon succumbed to the lumberjack's axe. In their wake, like tinder on the land, lay great stretches of "slashings" - tangled, withered masses of discarded trunks, tops, branches and pine needles - intermingled with a ten-year growth of poplar.

The Bay City *Morning Call* labeled the woods

as "dry as a man after eating salt mackerel." Yet many a farmer throughout the Thumb seeking to convert the forest to farmland continued to hew the big hardwoods, drag the logs into great windrows and set them afire. Throughout the month of August those mammoth bonfires repeatedly blazed out of control, threatening farmhouses and villages.

On August 5 the citizens of Bad Axe got quite a scare when a windstorm whipped a fire toward the village "in a tremendous cloud of smoke and flames that bid fair to devour everything in its path." Judges, lawyers and even prisoners on trial emptied the big brick Huron County Courthouse and ran for their homes. But suddenly the wind changed direction and the danger passed. The Bad Axers might have taken that dress rehearsal to heart and made preparations for the big show to come, but, instead, congratulated themselves on their good fortune and did nothing to protect the town during the following month as other fires billowed to the south and west.

On September 4, Sunday afternoon, 21-year-old Roderick Park learned that a clearing fire had gotten out of control ten miles to the west of the village. He joined a party of young men sent out by the landlord of the Bad Axe Hotel to fight the blaze. They arrived at dusk to find a "great spectacle" and one truly out of control. Realizing "there was nothing that human hands could do to stop it," they returned to town.

Park and the rest of the villagers rose for business as usual the next morning, little suspecting that the brisk west wind had awakened a dragon. At mid morning the wind increased in velocity. By noon it blew with hurricane force, tearing off roofs, splintering log cabins, hurling people through the air. In southeastern Huron County a thousand-pound wagon flew 245 feet across the railroad tracks. Elsewhere, big boulders "rolled along the ground as if they were pebbles." The tempest fanned the brush fires into hundred foot high sheets of flame that outran steam locomotives.

Billowing clouds of smoke that blotted out the sun preceded the racing fires. To the southeast, a Minden resident related: "The smoke began to roll over us about ten o'clock. At noon we had to light our lamps to see to eat our dinners. At three o'clock we had to light lanterns to see in the street. At times the darkness was so intense that we could not see anything, and then occasionally everything would be lighted up by a red glare that would give the buildings and trees the appearance of red blood."

In Bad Axe, amid the stygian darkness citizens heard a "horrible roaring" about 1 o'clock, and then flaming brands began raining down on roofs. Within ten minutes, nearly the entire village went up in flames as if from spontaneous combustion. Some 400 people groped their way to the only brick structure, the big mansard-roofed courthouse. Women and children huddled terror stricken on the floor of the refuge while 30 or so men battled the flames in the business block across the street that threatened to ignite the courthouse. Pumping water from the courthouse well, others formed a bucket brigade to wet down all they could reach of the structure's exposed wood. A lawyer's wife laboring as part of that brigade spotted a minister "kneeling with his flock, imploring the help of the creator." She told him he should pump now and pray later. The reverend dutifully rose from his knees and pitched in, "no doubt praying as he pumped."

The men fighting the fires in the business block could stand the intense heat for only minutes at a time. When the fire reached the gunpowder and 30 barrels of kerosene in the hardware store the heat became unbearable. Everyone retreated inside the courthouse, and then came the time to pray. Although windows buckled and cracked with the heat, miraculously, the brick walls held. The villagers emerged hours later to find nothing but ashes, "the tract could have been plowed as

An artist for *Leslie's Illustrated* executed a woodcut of a family fleeing the Thumb fire of 1881.

a farmer prepares his ground for sowing seed." But they were alive!

Not so fortunate were many other Thumb residents as the inferno swept across Huron, Sanilac, Tuscola, Lapeer and northern St. Clair counties. Onrushing flames hurtled 50 to 100 feet in the air, lunged forward to cremate everything before them, then like a bouncing ball rose for another leap. Amid the devastation lay islands of forest untouched as the flames arched high over them.

The pitch blackness that preceded the flames worsened the situation. Dazed and confused, many victims dashed blindly into the thick brush rather than open fields. Others fled to the east, wrapped in wetted bedding. Several families took refuge in wells. Two miles south of Ubly, Dennis O'Connell, his wife and eight children lowered themselves into a 12-foot-deep well with a couple feet of water at the bottom. Three members of a neighboring family joined them. The thirteen persons stood cramped, in utter darkness and nearly suffocated from smoke, for five hours until they dared venture out to view the havoc.

In Sanilac County, John and Mary Freiburger and their eight children also squeezed into a well. They were found days later, dead of suffocation.

One of the deadliest areas was Parisville, a farming community settled by Polish immigrants. Men, women and children, 22 in all, perished in a few minutes time.

On foot and by the wagon load, refugees with cinder-burned clothes and singed hair retreated before the flames to wade into Lake Huron. Bears, deer and other wild creatures stood amongst the humans. Sailors seven miles out on the lake felt uncomfortable warmth on their faces. The intense heat baked potatoes in the ground and corn on the stalk two miles away.

Within an hour after mailman Humphrey rode north from Marlette, he found himself in a race with death, and the wall of flames was gaining on him. As flaming cinders fell from the sky, the woods on either side ignited. Humphrey knew his route well. About a mile ahead lay a big open field where he thought he could find sanctuary. Suddenly he came upon a woman and her daughter wrapped with wet blankets, stumbling forward in terror.

Knowing they were doomed without his help, he reined his mount, leaped off, lifted the two to the saddle and and swatted his horse's rump. Though the horse suffered a badly burned mane and tail, the women made it to the field and survived. A rescue party found Humphrey's charred body on the road, draped over his saddlebags in a last gallant effort to save the mail.

When the conflagration finally hissed out in Lake Huron, Huron City, Charleston, Ubly and Tyre were gone. The official death toll for "the worst day in the Thumb's history" reached 282 - many other missing victims certainly perished also. In a matter of four to five hours, more than one million acres and 3,400 buildings lay in smoking ruin. Relief efforts sprang up across the state to assist the 15,000 homeless refugees.

Nationally circulated periodicals carried news of the holocaust to Dansville, N.Y., where America's original Red Cross chapter had been initiated three weeks before. Clara Barton immediately launched a campaign to help victims of "Michigan's Terrible Calamity," the first such effort by the American Red Cross.

How Carp Came To Michigan

Eli R. Miller peered into the murky pond on his farm northeast of Richland one spring day in 1885. Spying big dorsal and wagging tail fins, he jabbed hard and yanked up a hefty carp wriggling on his trident. Miller marveled at how large his piscine prize had grown in the four years since he stocked the pond with minnows. The old pioneer, who had carved out a homestead a half century before, rubbed his palms at the prospect of the profits to be harvested from his carp farm.

Later that evening, he sat down to enjoy the big baked fish steaming on a platter. Thoughtfully chewing a mouthful, Miller found the flesh coarse and bland save for a distinct muddy flavor. Pushing back his plate, with a frown he pondered how a dish so praised by European gourmets could taste so bad.

During the last quarter of the 19th-century, Miller and many another deluded American considered themselves on the cutting edge of pisciculture. Beginning in the 1870s, zealous federal and state bureaus had touted the importation of carp as a panacea for the ailing shad, salmon and Great Lakes whitefish industries. Technical articles on the potentially huge profits to be reaped from carp culture, and translations of works by Germans, the leading European carp fanciers, such as Max von den Borne's "Raise Carp!," further fanned the fad. Unfortunately, few of those caught up in the fish fever took the trouble to taste the finny product - and there lurked a problem.

Commonly called German carp, the species actually originated in Asia. The ancient Chinese crowned them "king of fish" because of their strength, durability and amazing powers of procreation, the very traits that would bring condemnation in America. By 475 B.C. the Chinese raised carp in ponds, man's earliest attempt at fish culture.

Prior to the 13th-century, carp spread to the Middle East, probably via Chinese traders. Soon after, crusading knights brought pepper, garlic, watermelon and carp back to Europe from the Holy Land. By the beginning of the 19th-century the Danube and other slow-flowing, muddy European streams teemed with wild carp. The insatiable demand for the big herbivorous fish led to the development of an intensive carp raising industry that supplemented commercial fishing operations. During the 1870s, Berliners alone consumed more than 500,000 pounds of carp annually.

In 1871, the federal government created the United States Fish Commission, headed by Professor Spencer Baird, renowned ornithologist and later director of the Smithsonian Institution. Baird embraced the concept of carp as a valuable substitute for vanishing American species and, when raised in ponds, as a supplemental source of income for farmers. In 1877, he ordered the first shipment of carp from Germany. Two years later the federal government began distributing the fecund breeding carp to the numerous state fish commissions clamoring for the highly recommended newcomers.

Michigan had created a State Board of Fish Commissioners in 1873 to oversee the artificial propagation of whitefish. It soon expanded its role to attempt to stem the extermination of grayling and other rapidly disappearing native fish and to introduce exotic species including eels, salmon and rainbow trout.

Carp seemed a natural candidate for the state's streams. In November 1880, the commission procured "20 pair" of government minnows from Goshen, Indiana. The fish found a new home in a quarter-acre pond at the state fish hatchery near Pokagon, between Dowagiac and Niles. The Hoosier carp thrived, growing to 17 inches and three and a quarter pounds within 13 months. When the state fish hatchery moved to

Dutch entrepreneurs netted more than 86 tons of carp from Holland's Black River in 1912.

Paris, Mescosta County, the Pokagon carp wound up in some private ponds at Glenwood, 12 miles to the north. By the spring of 1884 they had reached a weight of 13 pounds.

That year, Rolla C. Carpenter, professor of mathematics and civil engineering at the Michigan Agricultural College in East Lansing, constructed a series of ponds on the river flats adjacent the campus. The State Fish Commission, it seems, had convinced the State Board of Agriculture that the culture of carp, the "farmers' fish," would form a logical addition to the college curriculum. Although smaller ponds at the college's botanical garden were stocked with minnows, the East Lansing carp experiment was mysteriously aborted. Nevertheless, the State Board of Agriculture continued to promote carp culture, publishing, for example, lists of plants suitable for growing in ponds as carp food. Carp did well on manna-grass, duckweed and wild rice, but, the board warned, bladderwort, an insectivorous plant, itself fed on carp fry.

Sportsmen joined the farmers in welcoming the German immigrants to the state's waters. Richland's Miller, who had become such an advocate of carp farming that he was appointed to the State Fish Commission, delivered a paper on the carp program to the annual meeting of the Michigan Sportsmen's Association at Bay City in 1882. Although neither Miller nor anyone else present had yet tasted carp, based on Baird's recommendation that "carp is better than any other fish in the Potomac," including black bass, the sportsmen gave tacit approval of the project to stock Michigan's rivers and lakes with the big fish.

But as the 19th-century drew to a close, came a decided reaction against the whiskered monsters that thrashed the shallows of the state's streams in increasing numbers each spring. Sportsmen branded carp nuisances that were replacing the highly coveted black bass population. The vegetarian fish, which took the hook only when a baited by a doughball, held little appeal for anglers. Worse yet, many Americans found carp's coarse, muddy taste repugnant and blackballed the species as "trash fish." In reality, that aversion stemmed from failure to practice proper preparation techniques.

European cooks routinely steeped the live fish in a tub of fresh water for several days to cleanse the muddy taste, then marinated the fish in milk, brine or beer. They seasoned its bland flesh with onions, garlic, hot pepper, thyme, plenty of butter or lard and served the dish with piquant sauces. Eastern European Jews enjoyed carp as spicy gefilte fish, a traditional Sabbath dish accompanied with horseradish relish. Other popular European recipes included boiled, grilled and baked

Allegan's master newspaperman Joe Armstrong photographed acres of carp killed by industrial pollution near Dumont Creek in 1953.

carp, fish patties, carp in jelly and sweet Polish carp. But to most Americans those foreign dishes held little appeal compared to planked whitefish, broiled trout or fried pan fish.

Distaste deepened for the turgid plant eaters that sometimes grew to 90 pounds or more. In 1911, the Michigan legislature passed an obnoxious fish ordinance, citing carp as the primary culprit. In an attempt to eradicate carp the state began awarding obnoxious fish contracts to commercial fishermen. Holland area entrepreneurs responded by netting more than 86 tons of carp from Lake Macatawa in 1912 alone.

Such efforts brought little long-term relief. Rivers like the Kalamazoo became prodigious spawning grounds for carp. The situation drew national attention in 1953 via an award-winning photograph by Allegan ace newspaperman Joe Armstrong of acres of floating carp killed by hydrogen sulphide pollution in the Kalamazoo River.

But enough carp survived that and other industrial poison spills during the 1950s and 1960s to maintain a burgeoning population. And while grayling, passenger pigeons and other once dominant native fauna are no more, carp and many another alien invader unleashed on Michigan's environment have established permanent niches.

Father Francis O'Brien, Renaissance Man

They called him Father Frank, Monsignor Francis A. O'Brien and "The Catholic Genius of Kalamazoo." During four decades of community leadership he established an amazing variety of pioneering medical, charitable and educational institutions in Kalamazoo. Governors and presidents sought out his expertise. An able newspaper editor and historian, he founded the Michigan Historical Commission. In 1913, a newspaper reporter wrote: "No field of human endeavor open to the priest has Father O'Brien not entered and in none has his influence not been convincingly felt." In short, the church leader best known as the founder of Kalamazoo's Borgess Hospital was a modern "Renaissance Man."

Born in Monroe, Michigan, on June 7, 1851, Francis Alphonsus O'Brien was the youngest of the five children of Irish immigrants Michael and Margaret O'Brien. Deeply religious, his parents inspired in their son a similar love for the Catholic Church. He received his early formal education at a local Catholic school. But when his father died in 1866, the 15-year-old dropped out of school to take a job in a Monroe grocery store to help support the family.

Over the following four years he earned a reputation as a keen business administrator. During a short stint as a Detroit *Free Press* reporter he honed his writing ability. But his real passion, the church, beckoned and through the assistance of his friends, Father Edward Joos of Monroe and Bishop Caspar Borgess of Detroit, he began to prepare for the priesthood.

He worked his way through Assumption College and the seminary at Mount St. Mary's of the West by teaching undergraduates. Ordained a priest in 1877, Father O'Brien served as a pastor at Monroe and Detroit before Borgess assigned his protege to

138

Kalamazoo in 1883.

The Kalamazoo parish which dates back to 1832 was genuinely in need of a strong leader. The church had been rocked in 1881 with the publication of former pastor Father B. L. Quinn's book, *Substitution For Marriage,* which alleged that priests were conducting a

Young Father "Frank" O'Brien, at about the time he took over the Kalamazoo Parish.

secret sex ring composed of new female converts.

O'Brien found a "church whose scandals had attracted the attention of the entire nation more or less in a dilapidated condition, the school and convent attached to it badly in need of repairs, the parish itself sunk in debt, and the majority of the parishioners wholly indifferent to the material condition of the church as well as their own spiritual condition." Father O'Brien zealously embraced his new challenge. His strong personality, diplomacy and sense of humor soon won him acceptance in the community. He began by placing the parish schools on a firm footing then launched a campaign to restore the St. Augustine Church.

In his limited spare time, he pursued scholarly activities. He delivered a brilliant paper on Catholic charities to the State Board of Charities and Corrections in 1885. Governor Russell Alger promptly appointed him to the organization. While serving as a board member he recommended a series of reforms which the state eventually adopted. Soon thereafter, President Benjamin Harrison appointed O'Brien to the Examining Board of the West Point Military Academy.

In the meantime, O'Brien continued to devote most of his energies to fulfilling his dream of making Kalamazoo the "Catholic Center of the West." In 1885, he began campaigning to establish a hospital in the city. While in many respects Kalamazoo, whose approximately 17,000 residents had adopted a new city charter the year before, was a thriving progressive municipality, medical facilities remained primitive. Tight-fisted voters blanched at funding the estimated $30,000-$40,000 required to create a hospital. O'Brien proposed to the city council that he could establish a hospital for the bargain price of $5,000, but even that figure proved unpalatable. Clearly, Kalamazoo's first hospital could only come through private funding.

O'Brien persevered and, almost miraculously, a few days before Christmas, 1888, came a $5,000 check

Barbour Hall Cadets, Nazareth, Kalamazoo Co.

Barbour Hall cadets practice their cannoneering skills, ca. 1910.

from Bishop Borgess. O'Brien applied the money toward the down payment on an Italian-Revival mansion, the former residence of Dr. Moses Hill, situated on a block of land stretching between Portage and Lovell streets.

The cornerstone of an addition to the structure was laid on June 30, 1889. A week later, eleven Sisters of St. Joseph arrived from Watertown, New York, the culmination of O'Brien's search for a religious order to operate the institution. The sisters set to work with a flourish and on December 8, 1889, Borgess Hospital officially opened with 20 beds and a staff of eight physicians.

Continued funding for the hospital long remained a concern, as did the reluctance of local protestants to patronize it out of fear that the sisters might try to convert them on their sick beds. Still, O'Brien energetically tackled other needs as well. In 1891, he opened a new school building named LeFevre Institute. Two years later he launched a parish newspaper called the *Angelus* which under his editorship evolved into the Kalamazoo *Augustinian*.

In 1896, O'Brien purchased a 160-acre farm on Gull Road for $8,500. By the fall of 1897 Nazareth Academy, which would evolve into Nazareth College, opened its doors. Two years later the St. Anthony Home for Feeble Minded Children began in a converted farmhouse on the Nazareth site. Originally operated by the Sisters of St. Joseph for girls only, in 1910 a larger facility constructed in Comstock admitted boys as well.

Also at Nazareth, Barbour Hall, one of the first elementary boarding schools for boys in the country, opened with a class of 15 in 1902. From 1941 until it closed in 1979, it functioned as Barbour Hall Academy. In 1915, O'Brien established St. Agnes Foundling Home in a converted residence on Portage Street to provide for the needs of orphans.

As recreation from his many charitable and educational pursuits, O'Brien enjoyed the study of Michigan history. In 1885, he joined the Michigan Pioneer and Historical Society. Over the succeeding decades he found time to write historical articles on early missionary activities, the work of Michigan's Sisters of the Holy Cross during the Civil War and biographies of pioneer churchmen. His monograph on historic place-names of Mackinac Island remains a classic in the field. Father O'Brien persistently campaigned for a state agency responsible for Michigan's historical assets. In 1913, the Michigan Historical Commission was created and he served as its first president.

That same year saw O'Brien elevated to the rank of Monsignor in recognition of his many accomplishments. Although he suffered a painful illness during the last few years of his life, O'Brien pleaded with his doctor to: "Keep me going. I want to die in harness." While working on plans for a new boy's school, he died on December 19, 1921 in his room in the new hospital he had established four years before on Gull Road.

In 1915, fellow historian and long-time friend Edwin W. Wood had this to say about Father O'Brien: "Had his work been cast along military lines, he would have made a great general, in business, the system and genius given him would have made him a successful captain of industry; in the law, he would have been an eminent jurist, and in national and public matters he was endowed with attributes sufficient to have made him as great a Secretary of State as the United States has ever had."

Joseph Bert Smiley:
Poet With A Punch

Galesburg's self-proclaimed poet laureate, Joseph Bert Smiley, was not a man to trifle with. In an era when western gun slingers dueled down dusty streets, Smiley's weapon of choice became vitriolic verse. Adversaries foolish enough to challenge him faced a verse monger who would sonnet them up one side and ode them down the other. But behind the lilting lyrics, cutting couplets and bardic bravado beat an unhappy heart destined for tragedy.

The eldest of the three children of George and Nora Smiley, Joseph was born in 1864 in the upper Mississippi River town of Anoka, Minnesota. The following year the family settled in Kalamazoo. A frail child who stammered and suffered from a nervous condition then termed St. Vitus Dance and now known as chorea, Smiley did not attend school until he was ten.

The special care his mother lavished on her sickly child wrought a deep lifelong bond. But that maternal solicitation could not protect from the cruel taunts with which children customarily assail anyone different. Proud and intelligent, Smiley learned to fight back with barbed wit and sarcasm against classmates who ridiculed his ailments. Poetry in particular became his passion and he reeled off juvenile jingles that cowed many a bully. Not only did he win respect, but in 1884 he graduated from Kalamazoo High School as class president.

That fall he enrolled in the University of Michigan, but ill health forced him to withdraw within the semester. He recounted his one and only attempt at higher education in a humorous poem, "Ann Arbor:"

Full many classmates left our ranks
Before we'd scarce begun.

144

Some left who couldn't do the work,
And several got the run;
And others left because they flunked,
Some had to go away,
But the honest reason why I left
Was 'cause I didn't stay.

Armed with three months of university education and an ever-growing sense of his poetic "divine afflatus," Smiley gravitated to newspaper work. His

Joseph Bert Smiley included his portrait as a frontispiece to *Nora* **published in 1895.**

first job, as a reporter and local editor of the Battle Creek *Moon*, brought the 20-year-old a salary of $6 per week. But when Smiley allotted less time to his daily assignments than to the reams of verse he published under the pseudonym, Samwell Wilkins, he got sacked after four months.

Moving back to the family home in Kalamazoo, Smiley eked out a livelihood by publishing programs for the Academy of Music on Rose Street. He also continued to scribble lyrics. A poem he published in the Kalamazoo *Gazette* in 1885 lamented the local lack of appreciation for his art:

> *When the editor's a prey to indigestion, indigestion,*
> *And his liver isn't working worth a cent, worth a cent,*
> *When he gives a gruff reply to every question, every question,*
> *And in grumbling o'er his woes his time is spent, time is spent—*
> *Then the poet makes some verses, and he writes 'em, and he writes 'em,*
> *And he brings 'em to the office when they're done, when they're done,*
> *And the editor takes a club and smites 'im, club and smites 'im—*
> *Oh the poet's lot is not a happy one, happy one,*
> *The poet's lot is not a happy one!*

In 1886 a rival newspaper, the Kalamazoo *Daily Herald*, started up with Smiley as its local reporter. Assigned to cover a city council meeting, he dashed off a long poem that poked good natured fun at the solemn proceedings. Smiley lasted only a few months at the *Herald*.

Next came stints with the Ottawa, Illinois, *Free Trader* and the Joliet *News*, both terminated for the usual reasons, "too much poetry."

In the meantime, Smiley published in 1886 a collection of his newspaper poems and short prose fancies as *Meditations of Samwell Wilkins*. He took to the road, pounding on doors across Michigan to hawk his 123-page, hardbound volume at a dollar. He succeeded in selling nearly 3,000 copies. His second volume, *A Basket of Chips*, appeared in 1888. Sprinkled among parodies of famous poems and other light-hearted lyrics appear a number of pieces about Kalamazoo happenings. Typical of Smiley's jibes at his home town is a stanza from a poem descriptive of the city:

> *The Michigan Insane Asylum*
> *Is up on the top of the hill,*
> *And some irresponsible crazies*
> *Meander around at their will,*
> *And they frequently talk to a stranger,*
> *And they sometimes escape, it is true,*
> *But the folks are not all of them crazy*
> *Who hail from fair Kalamazoo.*

Aside from the several thousand patients at the State Hospital, the city that Smiley tweaked was a vibrant community flexing its industrial muscles in the 1880s. Popularly known as the "celery city" because of vast acreage of the crunchy vegetable, its other major sources of revenue included iron foundries, buggy factories, windmill plants and the newly formed Upjohn Pill and Granule Co. The city's first telephone exchange had opened in 1881, the first electric power plant five years later, and in 1884 horse-drawn street cars clip clopped along busy downtown streets.

Then on May 8, 1889, came the worst tragedy the city had yet experienced. A speeding Michigan Central Railroad switch engine smashed into a steetcar on what is now Michigan Avenue, killing five women passengers and injuring six more. Among the horribly mutilated victims lay Smiley's beloved mother, Nora. That loss left a void that would never be filled.

Following the funeral, Smiley went back to his newspaper postion in Illinois and took refuge in his poetry. In July 1890, he returned to Kalamazoo where he launched an unsuccessful little newspaper he dubbed *Smiley's Weekly*. That fall he bought a flailing weekly in Galesburg he renamed *Smiley's Kalamazoo County Enterprise*. Smiley featured his poetry and other pithy sayings in each issue, and the community responded by increasing circulation.

But each issue saw less news reporting and more of the editor's personal views and biases. In poetry and prose he weighed into any who displeased him. He launched vituperative campaigns against local bankers and lawyers, the Galesburg postmaster, the village clerk and others. He crossed pens with Francis Hodgman, a Climax surveyor and poet, and the two publicly flayed each other in rhymed repartee.

In 1893, the handsome young editor began courting Nina Burdick, the daughter of a prominent Galesburg physician. Her mother, Lucinda, objected because of Smiley's nervous twitching and broke off the match. The embittered suitor retaliated by writing, "St. Peter at the Gate," a ballad about a shrew resembling Lucinda who was refused admittance to heaven while her husband was ushered in because he had already suffered the tortures of hell during his long marriage. Published in the *Enterprise* and later in pamphlet form, the piece became a national best seller and the one poem of Smiley's that has survived in numerous anthologies.

In 1895, Smiley delivered Lucinda the coup de grace via his third publishd book, *Nora*, a long epic poem about the unjust jilting of a suitor through the machinations of a jealous mother.

Having evened his score with the Burdicks, Smiley courted and in 1896 married Fern Hawks. Ten months later she bore them a daughter they named Nora. But even as he seemed to find contentment in his domestic role, Smiley continued to slash with poetic polemics Galesburg's leading citizens. When he attacked the Galesburg superintendent of schools, citizens held a mass meeting and hanged Smiley in effigy. As the decade wore on and his antics alienated more and more townspeople, the *Enterprise's* circulation dwindled.

By 1902 the situation had reached a crisis. Financial difficulties and local ire forced him to move his family and the newspaper office to Augusta. A few months later he suspended publication of the *Enterprise*. Suffering a nervous breakdown, he checked into a Battle Creek treatment center. The sanitarium brought little relief and Smiley separated from his family. On the 14th anniversary of his mother's death, May 8, 1903, Smiley put a bullet in his brain.

His last rhyme writ, his 38-year-long battle against the odds was over and he had lost. Yet, ironically, none of Smiley's many adversaries, save Climax poetaster Hodgman, enjoy monuments to their memories as enduring as the slim volumes of verse coveted by collectors that still turn up in area antiquarian book shops.

The Great English Sparrow Hunt

During the first three months of 1898, Kalamazoo County Clerk William A. Forbes counted so many bird heads that he had nightmares about sharp little beaks. Up in Allegan, County Clerk Charles L. Barrett grew queasy when he peered out his window of the grand Romanesque courthouse that dominated the city's architecture to spy a covey of hunters with burlap bags slung over their shoulder slogging toward his office. Van Buren County Clerk Joseph S. Buck took a long vacation that winter to escape the boxes, bags and bushel baskets of the tiny sparrow heads that had peeped their last. In Coldwater, Branch County Clerk Burt M. Fellows fingered through more than 53,000 of the gruesome trophies. But Gratiot County Clerk Hiram Harding took the prize. He counted 190,230 heads and diligently paid two cents apiece to the bounty hunters. And so it went across the peninsulas as the State of Michigan waged relentless warfare against the hated avian invaders known as English sparrows, now simply as house sparrows.

Like so many of the ways mankind has mucked up the natural order, the introduction of sparrows began with good intentions but bird-brained thinking. Reasoning that the continent could be improved by adding to the indigenous bird life a European species fabled in song and story, groups and individuals across the nation began importing breeding pairs.

New York City's Brooklyn Institute pioneered the sparrow craze in 1850. Those first immigrants did not thrive, but the institute persevered and in 1852 another batch was carefully nurtured. Released the following year, the fecund fowls that bred nestfuls three or more times a year quickly spread throughout the city and then winged north, south and west.

Others, too, wanted their share of sparrows, and

over the next decades citizens established colonies in Portland, Maine; Galveston, Texas; Cleveland, Cincinnati and San Francisco. In 1869, Philadelphia officials turned loose a thousand sparrows on the "city of brotherly love."

In the early 1870s, George S. Cowan of Monroe brought the pioneer sparrows to Michigan. By 1875, citizens of that old French city enjoyed the company of several thousand of the "noisy, chattering, pugnacious, restless sparrows." Ann Arbor and Jackson got their first sparrows between 1874 and 1875. The following year a fancier liberated four birds in Owosso. In 1880, the Kalamazoo *Gazette* noted that the "industrious little birds have taken possession of Main Street." The birds spread fast and by the end of the decade had taken up year round residence over most of both peninsulas, including Beaver Island and Mackinac Island. In the Upper Peninsula's Iron Mountain a resident recorded, "like the poor they are always with us."

European bird dealers appreciated the steady stream of eager American buyers, yet many must have scratched their heads in wonder. None of the importers, it seems, had taken the trouble to research the habits of the sparrows. They might, for example, have queried some of the sparrow clubs that had sprung up as early as 1744 in practically every English parish. Those neighborhood organizations existed for the sole purpose of destroying sparrows and their eggs because the birds were a well-known threat to crops.

Again without doing their homework, other American fanciers began importing sparrows to help control caterpillars and other harmful insects. Unfortunately, house sparrows rarely eat bugs, but they do relish grain and the buds and blossoms of fruit trees. Having secured numerous footholds in America, the sparrows found the republic the land of opportunity. They thrived particularly in urban areas, growing fat and sassy from grain spilled at elevators and by scratching out the partially digested oats in the horse manure that littered city streets. In the fall, ripened fields of waving grain made for easy pickings.

Before long, folks began to notice other unpleasant traits. The birds liked to build ramshackle nests in building cornices, rain gutters and ivy covered walls. As the ever-growing flocks roosted, they plastered all below with acidic droppings, destroyed ornamental vines and dammed up gutters and downspouts. The feisty sparrows attacked and drove away beloved native species such as bluebirds, wrens, tree swallows, purple martins, robins, chickadees and flycatchers.

Soon, agricultural scientists added other blots to the birds' record. When they lined nests with feathers from poultry yards they spread chicken mites and lice.

The little avian alien that inspired so much hate.

And when they wallowed for bits and pieces of food in pig pens, the mud carried away on their feet dispersed the dreaded hog cholera.

By the mid 1880s the once beloved house sparrow had few friends left. Albert J. Cook, a professor of entomology at the Michigan Agricultural College in East Lansing who compiled a guide to Michigan birds in 1893, listed as synonyms for English sparrows, "parasite, tramp, hoodlum, gammon."

A few miles from the college campus, Michigan's legislative leaders had already weighed into the sparrow strife in no uneven terms. In 1885, came a law stripping from English sparrows the statutory protection afforded other song birds. Two years later, the state enacted a bounty law allowing one cent apiece for sparrows in lots of not less than twenty-five. The heads were to be turned in for verification by township or county clerks during the first three months of the year only, when most native species had migrated south. In 1889, a legislative act bumped the bounty to two cents for lots of ten or more. The great Michigan sparrow hunt was on.

In an era when factory workers counted themselves lucky to earn ten cents an hour, the sparrow bounty gleamed as a feathered treasure trove. Some took to sniping the little songsters with small bore rifles, slingshots and new fangled "Daisy" BB guns manufactured in Plymouth, Michigan. Others laid out grain in long windrows and when the quarry alighted fired a raking double-barreled shotgun blast. A few sportsmen tried fine-mesh clap nets similar to those used to capture passenger pigeons by the millions.

But the cagiest of the hunters favored chemical warfare. Two schools of thought emerged. The first championed scattering a bed of strychnine-soaked grain which slew the sparrows that consumed it in a matter of minutes. Many of the birds, however, tended to be frightened off by the death throes of their poisoned comrades. So other bounty hunters used grain dusted with arsenic, a slower acting agent that permitted the whole flock to fill their crops before they began to drop.

Of course, poisoning the birds had one major drawback - it rendered them inedible. It had not taken Victorian gourmets long to rhapsodize over the gustatory qualities of the little birds. New York City marketeers began offering sparrows at one dollar a hundred. A dozen could be purchased for a quarter, just the right quantity for a family-sized sparrow pie. Other cooks favored skewering the wee birdies, draping a bit of bacon across their breasts and basting them until golden brown to produce a feast of fowl to melt in your mouth.

Still other midwestern entrepreneurs cashed in on the passerine bonanza by selling great quantities of live birds to gun clubs. Before the advent of clay pigeons, trap shooters normally utilized passenger pigeons - but by the late 1880s the wild pigeons were getting rather scarce. Sparrows made tolerable substitutes, but the quick little targets often outwitted the marksmen, and thus were further broadcast across the land.

As the 1890s wore on, the Michigan sparrow bounty program, a measure adopted by not many other states, grew by leaps and bounds to strain county coffers. The bounties paid in Branch County jumped from $142 in 1894 to $1,064 in 1898. That year Jackson County paid out $2,370, Ingham County $2,407 and Eaton County $1,386. And what really galled was that the more money that was spent, the better the sparrow population prospered while the native birds grew scarcer and scarcer.

As it turned out, the sparrow bounty hurt the indigenous birds nearly as much as the sparrows did.

County and township clerks were no ornithologists, and among the sparrow heads they counted were those of thousands of red polls, gold and purple finches, tree sparrows and other superficially similar species.

And, as might be expected, corruption reared its ugly head. In 1899, a hunter named Louis Gorsline collected sparrow bounties totally $5,706 from Isabella and Gratiot counties. An investigation resulted in Gorsline's and a deputy township clerk's arrest on the charge of conspiracy to defraud Isabella County. The case received widespread publicity as "the great sparrow caper" and dragged on until 1905 before being dismissed.

The sparrow caper and the gradual realization that the bounty had little effect other than feathering hunters' pockets spurred state lawmakers to rescind it in 1901. Michigan's sparrow population continued to soar until the 1920s when it began to spiral down. As automobiles replaced horses, the supply of second-hand oats diminished. Modern architecture offered fewer nesting opportunities. Then, too, intense competition came from another alien invader - the starling.

Once passionately hated and now accepted and enjoyed by many, the house sparrow has settled into its niche across America and Canada. It continues to nest in every one of Michigan's 83 counties.

When Freshwater Sailors Battled On The High Seas

Denby ducked when the Spanish shell hissed into the sea, sending high a splash that spattered the ship's stern. White puffs from the parapets of the ancient Morro Castle that guarded the harbor at San Juan, Puerto Rico, signaled the blast of more big cannons. Enemy ships swept forward and exploding shells bracketed the armorless American vessel.

Edwin Denby and the other 280 Michigan sailors manning the *USS Yosemite* were trapped like ducks in a shooting gallery. It was then that their commander, William H. Emory, gave the order - to attack!

Whipped to a patriotic frenzy by "yellow press" Spanish atrocity stories and the mysterious sinking of the *Maine,* thousands of Michigan youths eager to win martial glory rushed to answer President William McKinley's call to arms on April 25, 1898.

The state would "cut quite a figure" in the "splendid little war." Russell Alger from Detroit served as McKinley's secretary of war. Galesburg-bred "Big Bill" Shafter commanded the American army that invaded Cuba. Two of Michigan's five volunteer regiments fought there, more than those of any other state. And the exploits of the men of the Michigan Naval Brigade would show the world that freshwater sailors knew a thing or two about battling on the high seas.

Organized in 1896 as a branch of the state militia through the efforts of Truman Newberry and others, the Michigan Naval Reserve maintained stations at Detroit, Saginaw and Benton Harbor. Beginning, in 1897 the sailors trained on the *Yantic*, a three masted vessel launched during the Civil War. Assistant Secretary of the Navy Theodore Roosevelt, a friend of Newberry's, inspected the unit in Detroit in 1897 and was duly impressed.

The crew of the *Yosemite* posed on the vessel's spar deck in 1898.

Hours after war had been declared against Spain, Newberry received a long distance telephone call from Roosevelt asking if the Naval brigade could completely man a ship of war. "Yes, sir," Newberry responded. Roosevelt told him they would be assigned as a unit to the *Yosemite*.

In its hurried preparations for war, the Navy Department found it necessary to purchase an auxiliary fleet for its far flung operations. The Navy bought four ocean liners including the *El Sud* which it renamed the *USS Yosemite*. A coal-fired vessel capable of cruising at 16 knots, with a 5,000-ton displacement, the *Yosemite* was quickly converted. Ten five-inch and six six-inch guns bristled from her decks. The hull of the 408-foot ship was painted "fighting gray."

Amid sad partings from "mothers, sisters, wives and sweethearts" who believed the war would last at least two years, the Michigan contingent left Detroit on April 29. Eight days later, the men boarded the *Yosemite* at Newport News, Virginia.

The crew that walked up the gang plank was probably unique in naval annals. Nearly 75% were university graduates and they numbered some of the state's most influential young men of their generation. Mortimer E. Cooley, an Annapolis graduate and then dean of the University of Michigan College of Engineering, served as chief engineer. The entire graduating class in mechanical engineering followed their dean aboard the *Yosemite*, including Chief Machinist Charles B. King, who two years before had driven Michigan's first horseless carriage. Henry B. Joy, who later organized the Packard Motor Car Co., served as chief boatswain's mate. Watch and Division Officer Newberry would go on to serve Roosevelt as his secretary of the navy and win election to the U.S. Senate in 1918. Gunner's Mate Denby, a former University of Michigan football star, would become secretary of the navy under President Warren G. Harding.

In mid-May, the *Yosemite* steamed to Hampton Roads, Virginia. After two weeks of drill and gunnery practice, she headed south to the war zone. Assigned to escort a transport carrying a marine battalion en route to a beach landing at Cuba's Guantanamo Bay, the *Yosemite* bombarded the bay, the marines waded through the surf and the first U.S. flag flew over the Spanish island.

Following a dangerous mine clearing operation, the *Yosemite* was ordered to intercept the *Purisima Concepcion*, a Spanish steamer conveying rations from Jamaica to the army in Cuba. Through "some unexplained carelessness or bungling by the officers on watch," the *Yosemite* allowed the prize to elude her.

Smarting from that slip-up, the Michigan men vowed to redeem themselves on their next assignment. On June 26, the *Yosemite* relieved the *USS St. Paul* off the coast of San Juan, Puerto Rico. For the next three weeks she single-handedly blockaded the port. Opposing the Michigan detachment was the strongest fortress in the West Indies, Morro Castle, equipped with long range cannons. Anchored within the harbor sat two enemy cruisers, a gunboat and a torpedo boat.

Emory had been warned to keep a sharp eye out for the *Antonio Lopez,* which had sailed from Spain loaded with supplies for the troops on the island. At 5:00 a.m. on June 28, following a severe rainstorm the lookout in the crow's nest spotted a large ship silhouetted against the receding rain clouds about 14 miles to the west. As the vessel steamed at full speed for the harbor, the *Yosemite* gave chase.

The *Antonio Lopez* made it to within six miles of the sanctuary of the harbor before the *Yosemite* got within range. Twice Denby fired rounds across the ship's bow, but she continued to race for shore. Then the gun crews began blasting away with broadside after broadside. Unfamiliar with the waters, the panicked

Spanish vessel ran aground on a coral reef. The crew quickly abandoned ship as the *Yosemite* continued to pepper the stranded steamer with shot.

Suddenly, the cannons at the Spanish fort roared. Big shells that would have sliced through the armorless vessel's hull like a hot knife through butter threw up huge water spouts less than a hundred yards away. At the same time, the crew spotted three enemy vessels steaming hard from the harbor's mouth. The Spanish ships opened fire and shells landed in front, behind, left and right, some so close they swept the deck with water.

Swinging sharply, the *Yosemite* dashed straight toward the foe. The Wolverine gunners fired salvo after salvo. Denby recalled: "From stem to stern, the

The *USS Yosemite* in action at San Juan.

Yosemite was enveloped in choking smoke. The roar of the five-inchers and the bark of the six-pounders blended together - a concert of death dealing shells."

The Michigan marksmanship turned the tide of battle. Two shells slammed into the cruiser *Alfonso XIII*. Listing heavily she retreated back to the harbor. The other cruiser, the *General Concho,* turned tail as well. The smaller torpedo boat, the *Terror*, had been hit also. It limped along the coast, taking refuge behind the beached *Antonio Lopez*. The *Yosemite* turned to lobbing shells into the stranded vessel so as to totally disable its hull.

As suddenly as it had started, the fierce sea battle had ended. The *Yosemite* had come through unscathed. The Spanish had seen enough of the freshwater sailors' seamanship to not venture from the shelter of the harbor again. The Americans continued to blockade the port until relieved by the *USS New Orleans* on July 15.

Admiral William T. Sampson's stunning destruction of the Spanish fleet at Santiago brought a speedy end to the conflict. The men of the *Yosemite* ended their 116 days' service and returned to Detroit, where cheering throngs welcomed home their heroes. Martial honors secured, they pursued civilian successes.

Sadly, the vessel whose Michigan crew had "etched its name in the log book of famous fighting ships" went down in a typhoon near Guam in November 1900.

Trowbridge:
The Dam Story

Clad in knickers and high-laced boots, a broad-brimmed hat pulled down over his ears, William A. Foote paced nervously back and forth across Allegan County's Trowbridge Township Dam. It was a blustery late afternoon on September 20, 1899. Below the dam, the Kalamazoo River boiled and heaved high white billows. Angry water churned beneath the spectacular one-lane iron bridge at 26th Street, past leaning trees along the banks whose foliage hinted of the autumn majesty to come, then disappeared dappling around the bend. But Foote noticed little of this scenic grandeur; his mind remained focused on the task at hand - the pioneering experiment in long-distance high-voltage electrical transmission.

Nearly two hours before, Foote had given the signal to release the first flood of water through the penstock, powering the 2,000 horsepower generator and sending 22,000 volts along the 24 miles of iron fence wire toward the little plant of the Kalamazoo Valley Electric Company at the corner of Kalamazoo's Water and Edwards streets. And with long distance telephone service yet unheard of in rural regions, Foote still did not know if the venture in which he had risked so much was a success or dismal failure.

Foote was no stranger to risk-taking or to failure. Born in Adrian in 1854, he attended the local public school and then learned the miller's trade. He gravitated to Minneapolis where he worked in several of the giant mills that ground the wheat grown on the Great Plains into flour. There, he studied the state-of-the-art steel roller milling process.

Returning in the early 1880s to his home town and determined to launch his own water-powered milling enterprise, he convinced local financier James Berry to back him in a venture using stone rollers instead of steel. The novel idea proved a colossal failure.

In 1884, in an effort to secure some much-needed income he rented a portion of his mill to a company that held a contract to power Adrian's first dozen electric street lights. It installed a water-powered arc light generator in Foote's mill. Enthralled by the operation of this revolutionary machine that would some day power appliances and conveniences then undreamed of the, 30-year-old entrepreneur decided to cast his lot with electricity.

Berry, who had lost heavily in the milling scheme, wanted no part of this new venture. But Foote succeeded in borrowing capital from a wealthy farmer and constructed a small electric plant capable of powering six street lamps. With the assistance of his younger brother, James B. Foote, an engineering genius, the enterprise soon became profitable.

But the River Raisin at Adrian lacked sufficient flow to operate a high-speed generator. The Footes sold the plant and set their sights on producing electrical current through steam at Jackson. Two primitive power companies already in operation in Jackson had failed to generate much enthusiasm because of their lackluster performance. While Grand Rapids, Flint and Bay City had converted, in part, to electric street lights, Jackson still relied on gas lights lit each evening by "old lamp lighters."

William Foote, a master salesman, pitched a proposal to the Jackson Common Council: "There is no reason why this city should lag behind the other great and growing cities of this state. I ask your permission to erect poles, stretch wires, and place a few electric street lights on downtown thoroughfares. I am not, at this point, asking for a franchise, only for permission to demonstrate the superiority of my arc lights." The council approved the trial and in partnership with Samuel Jarvis, proprietor of a Lansing engine works, the brothers constructed a high speed generator which supplied "juice" to a series of "dishpan" street lights, featuring incandescent carbon points under big tin reflectors. The resulting illumination attracted crowds of gaping citizens, and the council quickly voted the Footes a franchise.

Next came Battle Creek, where, in 1886, the Footes set up an electric dynamo and in partnership with Jarvis organized the Battle Creek Electric Light and Power Company. That same year the Footes' Albion Electric Light Company secured a franchise to light that city's streets.

Despite fast paced development, the Footes' operation remained severely under funded, due largely to the natural economics of utilities requiring investment of large sums in construction before they recouped from consumers. One of the company's early employees, George Stecker, remembered working 12 hours a day, seven days a week for $25 a month. More than once he had to lend back to his boss on Monday the wages he received the Friday before. He soon learned not to spend much on weekends.

But the constant belt-tightening did not prevent continued growth. In 1895, the brothers took over the Ceresco Mill and Hydraulic Company in Calhoun County. The following year, the Footes determined to add to their holdings the Kalamazoo Electric Company, a coal-fired operation originated to provide power for the city's electric street cars that had replaced the horse drawn models in 1893.

While visiting Kalamazoo one summer day in 1896, the Footes and Stecker took a buggy ride to Allegan. The road then paralleled the Kalamazoo River much of the way, and they stopped frequently to survey potential water power sites. Between Plainwell and Allegan the natural flow of the river drops about 100 feet, a torrent by Michigan standards, and the brothers grasped the potential right away. If they could

Trowbridge Dam, Allegan, Mich.

The Trowbridge Dam, ca. 1909, harnessed the Kalamazoo River for the first long range electrical transmission.

establish generating stations at remote locations and devise a way to transmit power over relatively long distances to urban centers, a feat which had never been attempted, they had the makings of an electric bonanza.

The Footes wasted no time in laying the ground work for the big gamble. Teaming up with financier Charles Frisbie and engineer William G. Fargo, both from Jackson, they surveyed the region and began buying up vast holdings of land and riparian rights along the river between Plainwell and Allegan. They designated dam sites between Plainwell and Otsego, just below the confluence of Pine Creek and in Trowbridge Township.

Construction began on what Trowbridge residents called "the big dam" in the spring of 1898. Without bedrock to anchor the dam, a massive earth moving project resulted. Scores of muscular laborers wielded horse-drawn scrapers to scoop up the soil and pile it into huge mounds to temporally divert the river channel. They then heaped up and tamped tight another earthen barricade to dam up a pond 22-feet deep. Engineer Fargo designed an 80-foot-long spillway with three wooden gates and a 74 by 90-foot penstock, a pit for the wheel that drives the dynamo. A 90-foot-long wooden powerhouse rose above the penstock.

Running short of funds, the Footes decided to string on 20-foot-high poles cheap iron wire, instead of copper or aluminum, the 24 miles to Kalamazoo. If the experiment failed, they reasoned, they could at least recycle the wire as fencing. Lacking existing technology, Stecker, the project's chief engineer, had to invent a regulator to maintain a steady electric load and an oil filled "wagon box" type high-voltage circuit breaker.

When the momentous day arrived, a crowd gathered on the west bank of the river. William Foote and Stecker unleashed the pent-up power of the

Kalamazoo, the generator hummed, the wires crackled and a stream of electricity surged toward the Kalamazoo plant where James Foote stood by. Then came the long, agonizing wait. Finally, after two hours, a messenger on horseback galloped down the dusty dam road shouting, "The lights are working!"

The Footes bold wager had paid off big. Of course, problems surfaced. The following winter the iron transmission wire contracted in the cold and repeatedly snapped. But with the success of the Trowbridge Dam, the Footes found it easier to attract more investors, and they soon replaced the iron with aluminum wire. In 1900, the company extended the Trowbridge line to Battle Creek to provide power for the new electric interurban railway which linked that city with Kalamazoo.

In 1903, engineers stepped up the current from Trowbridge to 40,000 volts. By that date the Footes had also harnessed the river at the Plainwell and Pine Creek sites. In 1904, the Kalamazoo Valley Electric Company transmitted voltage 90 miles to Jackson. Within three years, from its Jackson headquarters the Footes' Commonwealth Power Company controlled the electric service in Kalamazoo, Battle Creek, Albion, Jackson and Grand Rapids.

In 1910, further consolidation yielded the Consumers Power Company, a vast conglomerate that emerged as Michigan largest utility provider with millions of customers in both peninsulas and tens of thousands of employees.

The wooden powerhouse at the Trowbridge Dam burned in 1911, to be replaced by a smaller brick structure. Its generator continued to feed electricity into Consumers' giant Michigan grid for 55 years. After decommissioning, the site was ultimately turned over to the Department of Natural Resources. A U.S. Marine Corps demolition team blew-up the powerhouse in 1974, and despite protests by Allegan County officials, the DNR destroyed the dam in 1987. Today, the only reminder of the vital role the Trowbridge Dam played in the pioneer days of electric transmission is a crumbling embankment and chute through which roar the unfettered waters of the Kalamazoo.

The remnants of the historic Trowbridge Dam in 1998.

When Vincent Price Said Tryabita

Vincent Price's forehead pulsed with pain - he was suffering a horrible headache - one monster of a headache. With the reputation and the fortune he had built up over four decades at risk, the stress of the situation was taking its toll.

No, the man stroking his balding temples in despair was not Vincent Price, the scary actor and gourmet cook, but his grandfather, Dr. Vincent Clarence Price, a Chicago-based baking powder tycoon. And the fall of the house of Price, which seemed only too imminent, stemmed from an ill conceived Kalamazoo County breakfast cereal venture.

The year was 1903. Kalamazoo was basking in the glow of its hard won reputation as the nation's Celery City. Generations of thrifty Dutch families had laboriously transformed the worthless swamplands that ringed the city into prime celery growing muck fields. Steam locomotives pulling boxcar loads of the crunchy commodity chugged out of the city to supply the nation's banquet tables with the traditional first course appetizer, "fresh as the dew from Kalamazoo."

At the same time, 20 miles down the Michigan Central Railroad tracks, rival metropolis Battle Creek was enjoying an economic boom also based on foodstuff - breakfast cereal. The roots of Battle Creek's rise to Cereal City are anchored in the Seventh Day Adventist Church. That sect, which made Battle Creek its world headquarters in the 1860s, had descended from the wreckage of upstate New York farmer William Miller's prophecy that the world would end in 1844. The ensuing "Great Disappointment" had galvanized diehard Millerites to form a new church based on the coming end of the world and the belief that Saturday should be observed as the Sabbath. Much of the Seventh Day Adventist dogma came from church

169

stalwart Ellen G. White, who periodically lapsed into trances to receive supernatural visions, then transcribing what had been revealed to her as "testimonials." One such vision in an Otsego farmhouse in 1863 decreed Adventists should practice vegetarianism. Other health visions advocated avoidance of tobacco, alcohol and spices as well as acceptance of the curative power of water. The Adventists opened the Western Health Reform Institute in Battle Creek, where rundown patients were treated to a bland vegetarian diet including rock hard Graham flour gems and fiendish medicinal baths, cold showers and enemas.

Understandably, patronage lagged at the water cure until a flamboyant young protege of the Whites', Dr. John Harvey Kellogg, took over its management in 1876. The diminutive doctor clad in a white suit reorganized the regimen, supplementing water treatments with other therapeutic procedures, launched a hectic building program and renamed the institute the Battle Creek Sanitarium, a name he had coined. By 1881, a staff of 80 doctors, nurses, cooks, masseurs and bath attendants catered to thousands of jaded clients who made the "San" their yearly health mecca.

Kellogg also tinkered in food reform, souping up the graham gems and gruel with the exotic foods he invented. His Savita, Protose and Nuttolene, which one guest likened to eating shoemaker's paste, were meat substitutes. Over the course of his long career, Kellogg also invented a caramel cereal coffee substitute, granola, peanut butter and in 1894 Granose, the world's first flaked breakfast cereal. Four years later, with the assistance of his younger brother and underpaid henchman, W.K. Kellogg, the doctor switched from wheat to corn to innovate corn flakes. The brothers eventually feuded over that product. In 1906, W.K. acquired control of the Battle Creek Toasted Corn Flake Company and from then on the signature on the package was his.

By then the Battle Creek cereal boom had become a national phenomenon - spurred not by Dr. Kellogg's health foods, on which he refused to spend advertising money, but by rival entrepreneur Charles W. Post.

A dyspeptic Texan, Post had checked into the Sanitarium in 1891 to seek relief from his stomach complaints. The treatments brought him little benefit, but he liked the doctor's health foods, especially the caramel cereal coffee and granola. Post opened up his nearby medical boarding house in 1892 and two years later began marketing his own coffee substitute, which he rather immodestly dubbed Postum. More important than the product he had cloned from Kellogg was Post's genius for advertising. By 1898 with the introduction of Grape Nuts, adapted from Kellogg's granola, total sales reached $840,000. Three years later, Post's annual advertising budget stood at $400,000, and he was clearing a profit of nearly $1 million a year.

Post's rise from rags to riches inspired scores of other incipient cereal czars to flock to Battle Creek from near and far. Approximately 80 different brands of breakfast cereals debuted during the first decade of the 20th-century. Imaginative entrepreneurs dreamed up bewildering variations of baked, flaked, chopped, mushed, shredded and impregnated wheat, corn, rice and oats and tried them on America's taste buds. A Battle Creek druggist compounded Cero-Fruito, wheat flakes sprayed with apple jelly. A local grocer called his cereal Per-Fo, short for perfect food. A homesick buckeye living in the Cereal City named his oat concoction Norka - Akron spelled backwards.

Benjamin Morgan, a Battle Creek realtor, came up with Golden Manna. Each box contained a prize, a ticket good for an automobile tour of his newly platted subdivision. A pair of mechanical minded brothers from Kalamazoo, Frank and George Fuller, created Korn Krisp. Unfortunately they left too much oil in the

The Paradise of Health

DR. V. C. PRICE

A Lecture by Dr. V. C. Price, on the great problem before the American People today—

FOOD

The baking powder king who gave the world its first and only celery-flavored breakfast cereal.

flakes, the product molded on grocery shelves and before long the Fullers were back in Kalamazoo tinkering with transmissions. Other short-lived Battle Creek cereals included Maple-Flakes, Bordeau's Boston Brown Flakes, Grain-O, Grape Sugar Flakes, Malted Zwieback, Malt-Too, Malto-Vita, My Food, Flak-Ota, Cocoa Creme Flakes, Cereola, Egg-O-See and Frumenta, which tasted pretty good but its razor sharp edges cut consumer's mouths. Then as now, gimmicks and novel brand names seemed more important to success than ingredients.

Into this yeasty ferment of cereal kings and celery Dutch battling for their respective culinary empires strode Dr. Vincent Price. Born in Troy, New York, in 1832, Price had studied medicine under a local practitioner and then earned a medical degree from New York College in 1856, specializing in pharmaceutical chemistry. He hung out his shingle in Waukegon, Illinois, in 1861.

Shortly thereafter, he discovered a new chemical combination for baking powder, "at once healthful and adapted to universal use." In 1863, he left the world of pills, poultices and panaceas to form a partnership to manufacture Dr. Price's Pure Cream of Tartar Baking Powder. His Chicago-based baking powder business proved a bonanza. By 1884 when he bought out his partner, Price's 200 employees produced tons of baking powder each day at the six-story factory in downtown Chicago. In 1891, when Price sold out his interests, he had become a very wealthy man. Not one to rest on his laurels, he launched other food related businesses. Dr. Price's Fruity Dessert was a jello-like product. The Price Flavoring Extract Company searched the world for its quality vanilla, orange, almond, ginger, anise and celery essences.

Clearly Price was an entrepreneur intent on diversification, and that is when the Battle Creek cereal boom beckoned. But to compete with the many other imaginative cereal makers Price needed a unique gimmick. Perhaps it was his experience with celery essence or merely the geographic proximity of the celery and cereal capitols that gave him the idea. In any event, Price decided to manufacture the world's first celery flavored breakfast cereal at an old water powered mill conveniently located at Yorkville on Gull Lake, almost exactly half way between Kalamazoo and Battle Creek.

As strange as it may seem, Price was not the first businessman to sense commercial advantage in celery flavored foodstuffs. Far more than a crunchy appetizer, celery boasted a folk medicine reputation as a cure for nervous disorders and as a sexual stimulant. In the 1890s, a host of Kalamazoo manufacturers had merchandized celery flavored chewing gum, celery pepper, celeryade drops, celery bitters, celery crackers and Kalamazoo Celery and Sarsaparilla Compound, advertised as a cure for "fever and ague, all forms of nervousness, headache and neuralgia and a positive cure for female complaints."

A breakfast cereal that would fill your tummy as well as alleviate the dreaded "bearing down sensation" that patent medicine pushers warned of - Price knew he had a winning combination, if he could only come up with a suitable name. And that is when he had his second brainstorm: he would call his cereal Tryabita!

Price acted quickly to put his scheme into production. The doctor took the precaution of patenting his brand name and the Tryabita logo which pictured a young girl spooning down a bowl of the cereal, the scene framed by wheat sheaves and celery stalks. He then secured the old George E. Little mill south of Yorkville on the outlet stream of Gull Lake, known variously as Gull Creek and Lover's Lane, at a reputed cost of more than $100,000. Price added a brick extension to the mill, modernized the operation and installed an additional steam generator. By early 1903 the smokestack of the Tryabita plant darkened country skies as Price launched his venture.

The little community of Yorkville was hard pressed to provide lodging for the estimated 50 production workers Price hired. But citizens quickly converted their homes to boarding houses. Tryabita workers labored the typical ten-hour work days of the period. They dumped bags of wheat into big rotating horizontal cylinders where it was steam cooked. When the

Tryabita's logo featured a young consumer framed by
wheat and celery stalks.

kernels had been thoroughly softened, they were "peptonized and celery impregnated." The resulting flavored mash was poured out onto a conveyor belt which transported the mushy kernels through flattening rollers. An elaborate series of conveyors carried the flakes through baking ovens where they were evenly toasted on both sides. Sometimes, batches were accidently burned. Those ruined flakes proved popular with local hog farmers as feed. That is, until the celery salt content made the hogs sick. Price should have sensed a problem there, but instead he pushed for greater production. When the plant was operating smoothly, employees could turn out 3,100 boxes each day.

The old baking powder hawker knew well the power of advertising, and he placed promotions for his product in widespread media. A 1903 Illinois vs. Michigan indoor track meet program carried a full page advertisement for Tryabita, stating that it was "used exclusively at the varsity training table" - no nervous athletes at the University of Michigan in those days. *Mother Hubbard's Modern Cupboard,* a popular cookbook published in Battle Creek in 1903, featured numerous recipes containing local cereal products. There, nestled among directions for making Grape Nuts Cream Fritters, Korn Krisp Pudding, Per-Fo Salmon Loaf, Golden Manna Puffs and Malt-Too Pudding, lurked recipes for Tryabita Food with Meats and Tryabita Bread:

> *One pint milk, or milk and water, lukewarm; 1 teaspoonful of sugar and 1 of salt; 1 compressed yeast cake dissolved in 1/4 cup of water. Stir this into 1 1/2 pints of Tryabita Food and 1 1/2 pints of spring wheat flour, thoroughly mixed, adding more flour if necessary, so that it will make a stiff dough that will knead without sticking to the board. After*

it has been thoroughly kneaded, grease your bread-raising pan with a piece of sweet lard about the size of an egg, put in dough and let it raise until three times its size, then take it out and put it upon the board and fold down; place back into greased bread-pan and let raise again, and fold down the second time. Divide the dough into two equal parts, put into tins and raise to twice its size. Bake in oven from 30 to 40 minutes.

Tryabita bread may truly be called the "Staff of Life" as it contains all the nourishing qualities to make bone and muscle and feed the nerves. These qualities are nearly all lacking in ordinary white bread.

But apparently even such potent guarantees could not convince enough consumers to try a bite of celery flavored cereal. And Price's real headaches began with trouble on the plant's assembly line. It seems the weight of the flakes varied greatly from batch to batch, which fouled up the machine that measured the cereal into packages. Fern Carley, who operated one of the package sealers in the plant, later remembered how "some boxes would have a cupful in them and other would be running over. It just seemed as if there wasn't any efficiency left in the plant."

Price alleviated his headaches, not by consuming his own alleged nerve rejuvenating product, but by halting production of Tryabita within a year or so and swallowing his losses like so many other of the ephemeral Battle Creek cereal makers.

Determined to salvage something from his Yorkville venture, Price dreamed up another cereal: Dr. Price's Algrain Food, a combination of wheat, oats, rice and barley served hot like oatmeal. Production of Algrain limped along at the Yorkville plant until it closed for good in 1912. The man who dreamed of celery flavored riches died two years later.

The mill at Yorkville where Tryabita was made is long gone, but its dam continues to maintain the level of Gull Lake. And Vincent Price, the doctor's towering grandson, parlayed his talent for frightening people into a lucrative film career. He also authored a number of gourmet cookbooks in the 1960s - none of which contain any mention of celery flavored cereal.

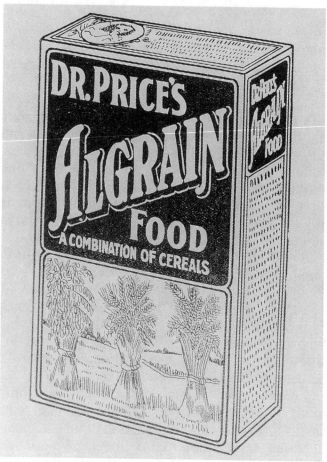

Dr. Price's second Gull Lake cereal proved little better than Tryabita.

Horseless Humor & Car-Toons

Did you hear the one about the motorist who died and approached the pearly gates:?

"Oh, let me in, kind saint,!" he cried,
But Peter said, "No, No!
You've brought your car; if you must ride,
There's cinder paths below."

It was 1905 - less than a decade since Charles King and Henry Ford had pioneered Michigan streets with their primitive horseless carriages - when an unknown joker penned that poem. It was an era when from many a pulpit rang more serious warnings about the evils of "devil wagons;" when physicians speculated that the human mind, and those of women in particular, could not remain balanced under the high speeds capable by some autos; when wild-eyed pedestrians scuttled out of automobiles' paths and teamsters shook angry fists as their steeds reared in terror.

In Battle Creek, Seventh Day Adventist Elder Uriah Smith thought he had solved the problem of equine trepidation when he mounted a wooden horse's head on the front of his auto. Smith was serious about his unlikely invention, but many other Americans simply greeted the noisy, smelly, speedy newcomers to the streets with that time honored Yankee tradition - jokes and laughter. Soon entire volumes with titles such as *Auto Fun* and *Chauffeur Chaff* lampooned autos and their drivers, with little apprehension that these rich men's toys and horses' enemies were even then in the process of revolutionizing American culture forever.

A number of standard themes gave birth to most automotive humor - accidents, for example. Tradition has it that Henry Ford set one of his many automotive precedents in 1896 when he and wife Clara ran over a boy on a bicycle, rendering the fortunately unharmed youth the first pedestrian to be struck by a car. Across Michigan the earliest automobile accidents achieved niches in local annals. Battle Creek experienced its first in 1902 when a local alderman lost control of his vehicle and plowed into a crowd, injuring five. Kalamazoo suffered its premier automotive fatality two years later.

Year by year, as more automobiles capable of greater speeds took to the highways, the automotive death toll rose exponentially. By 1922 Americans were annually killing 15,000 of their countrymen with their autos. Paradoxically, in the early days of motoring careless drivers' tendency to kill or maim humans, pets and livestock offered one of the most common sources of humor. Charles Welsh, a British writer of juvenile fiction who had settled in Scranton, Pennsylvania, edited *Chauffeur Chaff or Automobilia* in 1905. One of the earliest such compendiums, it featured numerous examples of such morbid humor as:

> *"Have you made a record with your automobile yet?*
> *"Oh, yes; two dogs, a chicken, three small boys, and a street cleaner, all run over in less than an hour!"*

Others of Welsh's selections made reference to recent world events such as the Philippine Insurrection where the American Philippine Constabulary battled guerrillas:

> *De Style: There were eight hundred killed in the Philippines*
> *Gunbusta: I didn't know they had automobiles out there.*

In 1908, Walter Pulitzer, a New York chess expert and song writer, the nephew of the wealthy newspaperman who funded the prestigious prizes

A ca. 1910 postcard depicted a pioneering motorist's bum luck.

named in his honor, published *My Auto Book,* a collection of his humorous verse, bon mots and parodies, interspersed with blank diary pages to record automotive outings. Under the diary heading "special incidents" he noted "killings can be omitted." Another of Pulitzers' jokes about vehicular homicide ran:

"I've had a streak of bad luck this week;
killed two men with my new touring car."
"Is that so unusual for you?"
"Well, no; but in this case one of the men
owed me a thousand dollars."

Even childhood rhymes offered Pulitzer a target for his murderous humor. He parodied *Mother Goose:*

Little Bo-peep,
She lost her sheep,
But of course she could not know
A big motor car
Had silenced his "baa,"
When it struck him a minute ago!

The craze for sending and collecting picture postcards that swept the nation during the first decade of the twentieth century offered another medium for deadly automotive humor. A 1908 example pictured a motorist stopping on a country road to greet a hunter and the dialogue:

Motorist: "Hello, killed anything?'
Sportsman: "No, have you?"

The cartoons featured in popular magazines of the period also frequently poked fun at motorists' mayhem. A typical example from 1915 showed a speeding automobile with the dialogue:

*Rider: "Why didn't you sound your horn when you
saw the man in the road?"*
*Driver: "I thought it would be more humane if
he never knew what struck him."*

Ranking next to accidents in popularity as a subject of automotive humor was the proclivity of the primitive vehicles to break down. As late as 1916, *The Motorists' Almanac,* produced by Massachusetts based magazine editor William Leavitt Stoddard, seriously cautioned readers that in April when they conducted their first tentative automobile tours of the season:

*Unless you are an old hand at it you are likely to
forget some of the spare things that make travel out
of town easy and comfortable. Be sure that you
have your wrenches, your pump and your extra
tubes and tire patches. ...A coil of wire is worth the
room it takes; so is a can of engine oil, and in case
a squeak or grinding starts up, it is good to carry a
squirt gun full of dope.*

A decade earlier *Chauffeur Chaff* had joked about the unreliability of autos:

"So you are going to get an automobile?"
*"Yes," answered the man who is always thinking of
his health.*
"My doctor says I must walk more."

Welsh's book also defined chauffeur as "a corruption of the term shover." Pulitzer adapted that theme to a parody of Omar Khayyam:

*A book of "Auto Rules" underneath the
bough,*

A stalled machine, a busted tire and Thou
Beside me lying in a slushy ditch.
Ah, slushy ditch were Paradise enow!

As automobiles threatened to replace America's traditional motive power, the horse, numerous comedians saw the humor of disabled vehicles requiring equine assistance. Pulitzer recorded one of many similar examples in 1908:

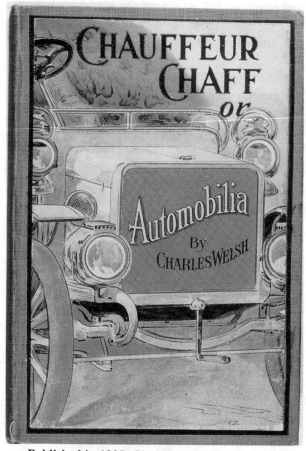

Published in 1905, *Chauffeur Chaff* was one of America's earliest collections of automotive humor.

First Motorist: My new machine is sixty horsepower.
Second Motorists: Isn't that stretching it a bit? Why only yesterday I saw two horses hauling it along the avenue!

Pulitzer also included a consolatory witticism that proved prophetic, considering the number of pleasure horses still kept by Americans:

The Cat: What's the matter, Mr. Horse? You look downcast.
The Horse: Well, haven't I cause? Since these blamed auto things have come into fashion, I feel that very soon I shall be put out of commission altogether.
The Cat: Oh, don't you worry. The mousetrap didn't put me out of business, did it?

The theme of romance in the automobile inspired many a punster to make use of the new vocabulary motoring brought to the language. In 1915, one unknown humorist quipped:

The automobile people to the contrary notwithstanding, the best sparking device continues to be a sofa, with the lights turned low.

Pulitzer, on the other hand, defined bigamy as "exceeding the speed limit in matrimony."

Muskegon raised Douglas Malloch, whose numerous books of woodsy poetry earned him the title "lumberman's poet," also saw humor in love a la auto:

Punctured
I wooed her the twentieth-century way,
With that wireless telegraphy known to all lovers.

In a trim automobile we rode out each day
And felt the same joy that the love ditties say
O'er a horse-propelled vehicle generally hovers.
But her father grew wrath when he saw my intent,
As fathers have often the habit of doing.
Now the vows are forgot and the auto for rent-
For to winter in Boston my darling he sent
And stopped all our automobiling and cooing.

Other themes that inspired humor include running out of gas, the smell of improperly adjusted gasoline engines (which assailed noses more used to the down-to-earth pollution left by horses) and the high cost of owning an automobile. Even Ransom Olds' little curved dash vehicle, one of the cheapest in the nation at $650 in 1901, was beyond the means of most working class Americans. A joke from 1905 ran:

"Why are you sure your wife will want an automobile for Christmas?"
"Why, there isn't anything that costs more, is there?"

Despite their relatively high cost the automobile caught the nation's heart and in hundreds of cities and sleepy hamlets monkey wrench inventors tinkered in backyard workshops to make their dreams of producing the best car for the price a reality. The number of American makes and models would eventually surpass 2,500. All but a handful would ultimately fall by the wayside, but in the years just before World War I the variety of makes on the market inspired Gelett Burgess, a humorist best remembered for his "Goops" books, to parody Lewis Carrol's "Jabberwocky:"

Motorwacky
'Twas metzger and cartercar

Did ford and fiat in the coles
All alco was kisselcar,
And the white winton olds
Speedwell the apperson, my son,
The marmon big, the pope adroit!
Oh, moon the michigan, and shun
The peerless paigedetroit!...

Today few other than automotive historians would recognize the names of the fifty cars Burgess cited in the seven stanzas of his clever poem. But in 1915, many a youngster could rattle them off. And it was in 1915 that an element of humor based on the "most famous automobile ever built" reached epic proportions: The Model T Ford joke. First marketed in 1908, the automobile that Henry Ford designed as "a car for the great multitude" had by 1915 achieved annual sales of more than 500,000 vehicles. Five years later, half the cars in the world were Model T Fords.

Affectionately dubbed the "Tin Lizzie" and the "fliver," the Model T was light, weighing around 1,000 pounds, simple enough in design for home maintenance, adequately powerful and built high enough to navigate the nation's notoriously rough country roads. Most importantly, it was cheap. The original price of $825 dropped to $260 for a touring car in the 1920s.

The factors that made the Model T so successful also inspired much of the humor centered around it. Because its low price appealed to blue collar workers, comics said: "A Ford will go anywhere except in society."

Its relatively small size coupled with its price inspired:

"Do you know what Ford is going to do now?"
"Paint his cars yellow so dealers can hang them in bunches and retail them like bananas!"

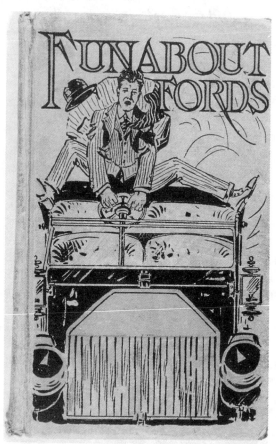

This 1915 publication was one of several that
codified hundreds of Model T jokes.

Its light and high-slung body, which naturally
caused it to bounce, gave rise to innumerable rattle and
shake stories:

> *"The Ford is the best family car. It has a tank for*
> *father, a hood for mother, and a rattle for baby."*
> and
> *"What shock absorbers do you use on your Ford?"*
> *"The passengers."*

The Model T's rough riding qualities led to tales that it routinely shed nuts, bolts and other parts along the road. And so they said:

"I hear they are going to magnetize the rear axles of the Ford."
"What's the idea?"
"So it will pick up the parts that drop off."

Another popular concept, that the Model T was constructed primarily of tin, formed the basis of many jokes:

A thrifty housewife saved all of her empty cans and shipped them to Detroit. After a few weeks she was delighted to receive the following letter.
Dear Madam: In accordance with your instructions we have made up and are shipping you today one Ford. We are also returning eight cans which were left over.

While most Model T jokes made the vehicle the butt of the humor a few testified to its more desirable attributes:

Why is a Ford car like a motion to adjourn?
Because it's always in order.

According to Mark Sullivan, chronicler of American social history of the first quarter of the 20th century: "The Ford joke was, even more than the Ford car, a staple, like sugar or salt, as familiar a part of the conversation of the American people from about 1914 to about 1918, as their shop talk, or sports, or weather." The prevalence of Ford jokes themselves even inspired some humor:

In a theatre the other night a man sat in his seat long after everybody else had gone. An usher touched him on the shoulder and said,

"The show is over mister."
'That can't be," was the reply,
"I haven't heard a Ford joke yet!'

Ultimately, like most things that get overdone, Model T jokes would run their course. J.J. White, who had compiled at least two booklets of Ford jokes by 1915, included one that hinted at the ultimate reaction:

"Have you heard the last Ford story?"
"I hope so."

Other forms of automotive humor would come and go to briefly tickle America's funny bone. The annals of popular culture groan with once timely jokes about Edsels, Nash Ramblers, Volkswagen Beetles, Pacers and Yugos, to name a few. And over succeeding generations, as automobiles evolved from an undependable plaything of the rich to an integral part of society, Americans continued to enjoy their unique sense of humor and laugh even harder at automotive foibles. By the way, did you hear about the display at the 1996 Greater Los Angles Art Show? Given the task of rendering a Yugo more useful, some creative New York City art students turned it into a giant pop-up toaster!

The Dowagiac Bishops & The Titanic Tragedy

The largest and most glamorous ship in the world had slid beneath the black waters of the North Atlantic. The hellish din of hundreds of drowning souls had faded. Now, the only sounds to break the crisp night's silence were the squeak of oarlocks and the splash of oars as the *Titanic* Lifeboat No. 7 groped its course over the glassy sea.

Huddled aboard were 12 women and 16 men, less than half the boat's capacity. Some shivered in the sub-freezing air. Others sobbed quietly as they grasped the reality that so many of their friends and relatives were gone forever. And with no rescue ship in sight, their own survival seemed anything but certain.

It was then that Helen Bishop, a beautiful 19-year-old newlywed from Dowagiac, attempted to buoy her shipmates' spirits with a story. On her honeymoon trip she had toured Egypt. There, a fortune teller had divined her future - she would survive a shipwreck and an earthquake before an automobile accident would end her life. "We have to be rescued," she laughed, "for the rest of my prophecy to come true."

The Michigan woman's odyssey had begun in November 1911, when she married Dickinson Bishop, a wealthy young widower whose first wife had willed him a major share in the renowned Round Oak Stove Company of Dowagiac. Helen, too, came from a well-to-do background. Her father, Jerrold F. Walton, had earned his fortune through proprietorship of the Sturgis-based Royal Easy Chair Company, whose prototype recliner was marketed under the motto "push the button and rest."

Early in 1912, the Bishops left their Dowagiac mansion for a three-month honeymoon tour of Egypt, Italy, France and other European attractions. They planned their itinerary to return on the highly touted

191

maiden voyage of the *Titanic*. On April 10th, at Cherbourg, France, they boarded the leviathan.

Nearly 900-feet-long and 94-feet-wide, the vessel's upper deck rose 90-feet above the water. The 29 boilers that powered the *Titanic's* three huge propellers and generated the ship's electricity each consumed more than a ton of coal an hour. Decorated with polished oak and mahogany paneling inlaid with mother of pearl, stained glass windows and a lounge resembling the palace at Versailles, the elegantly equipped ship boasted a swimming pool, turkish baths and a squash court. The Bishops were among the 190 first class passengers who paid the contemporary equivalent of $50,000 for their voyage. Second and third class bookings brought the total number of passengers to 1,325. Captain Edward J. Smith, a skilled skipper with 38 years of experience, commanded a crew of 898.

The White Star Line had widely promoted its new vessel as "practically unsinkable" because of its 16 watertight compartments that could be sealed off. When boarding, one passenger had asked a deck hand, "Is this ship really nonsinkable?" "Lady,"he answered, "God himself could not sink this ship!"

The *Titanic* steamed from Queenstown, Ireland, on April 11 for what was expected to be a routine and speedy voyage to New York City. En route, the Bishops enjoyed strolling the decks, playing bridge and rubbing elbows with other rich and famous first class passengers. They became friends with the fabulously wealthy John Jacob Astor and his young wife Madeline, Albert A. Stewart, an affluent New York printer, and John and Nelle Pillsbury Snyder.

On the afternoon and evening of April 14th, as the *Titanic* neared the Grand Bank south of Newfoundland, it received at least five wireless messages warning of icebergs. Capt. Smith opted to maintain his speed of 22.5 knots and rely on lookouts in the crow's nest to warn of danger. Unfortunately, those watches had not been issued binoculars. By the time they spotted a towering iceberg dead ahead it was too late to alter the course of the huge vessel fast enough. At 11:40 p.m., the *Titanic* struck the great mass of ice a glancing blow below the water line. The collision raked more than 200 feet of the hull. As steel plates buckled, the ocean gushed into five watertight compartments, flooded engine rooms and the big ship glided to a stop.

The Bishops had spent the evening partying in the lounge. They retired to their stateroom about 11:00

The lowering of the *Titanic's* lifeboats as imagined by an artist who was not there.

p.m. Helen was in bed and Dick reading when they felt the hum of the engines cease. Concerned, they dressed and made their way to the deck to see what was wrong. There, a steward assured them, "we have only struck a little piece of ice and passed it." The couple returned to their room, undressed and went to bed.

Before they could drift off to sleep, their friend Stewart pounded on the door, expressing concern about the list the ship had developed. "Get your wife, get dressed and go back on deck," he advised. Quickly dressing, they hurried to the life boat deck but saw no preparations being made to lower any of the 20 boats capable of accommodating 1,178 passengers. On the "A" deck, they encountered the Astors who seemed unalarmed. Feeling the cold night air, Helen asked for a muff and Dick returned to the cabin. He got the muff but left $11,000 worth of jewelry.

Back on the deck, they were ordered to don life belts. Still, few passengers yet realized the extent of their plight. They remained reluctant to board the life boats hanging 75 feet above the water. At the command, "put in the brides and grooms first," Helen was the first woman to be shoved into Lifeboat No. 7 and Dick followed. When the deck officer felt he could wait no longer, he ordered the half-loaded boat lowered at 12:45. The other boats followed, some with as few as 12 aboard. The last lifeboat to leave hit the icy water shortly after 2:00.

With only three crewmen aboard the Bishops' boat, some of the passengers, including Helen and a monocled British aviator, helped with the rowing. But Helen never forgot "the German baron aboard who smoked an obnoxious pipe incessantly and refused to pull an oar."

Fifteen minutes after the last lifeboat left the *Titanic*, Helen witnessed the end of the luxury liner. "For a moment," she recorded, "the ship seemed to be

A classic depiction of the last moments of the *Titanic*.

pointing straight down like a gigantic whale submerging itself head first." The tragedy claimed the lives of more than 1,500 people. Of the 32 from Michigan aboard, 19 survived, including three members of the Touma family from Dowagiac and four members of the Becker family from Benton Harbor.

The Bishops shivered for four hours in the life boat before being rescued by the *Carpathia*. When they reached New York, the couple testified before the Senate inquiry into the disaster headed by Dowagiac-born Michigan Senator William Alden Smith. The Bishops finally reached Dowagiac on May 10th.

Despite their survival of the colossal maritime calamity and their affluent lifestyle, the subsequent life of the Bishops would turn tragic. During a vacation trip to California a small earthquake jolted the couple - the second part of the Egyptian prophecy had come to pass.

While returning home from a party in Kalamazoo on November 5, 1913, Helen suffered a badly fractured skull in a automobile accident. She survived but with a silver plate over her brain. Her marriage deteriorated and she was granted a divorce in January 1916. Two months later, Helen slipped on a throw rug while visiting a friend's house and bashed her head near the silver plate. She died days later of cerebral hemorrhage. The front page of the Dowagiac *Daily News* carried her obituary on the left column. On the far right appeared the notice of Dick Bishop's marriage to Sydney Boyce, daughter of a Chicago publishing magnate.

But Bishop's life and those of many of the other men who survived the *Titanic* would also be tainted. For decades after, he endured the whispers and pointed fingers of a community that unjustly branded him the coward who dressed up like a woman to board a lifeboat on the *Titanic*.

The "Bare Torso King" In Battle Creek

America's most flamboyant strong man, Bernarr Macfadden, the mentor of Charles Atlas whose muscular metamorphosis inspired generations of 97-pound weaklings, liked little better than to show off. But on the cold winter night in 1908 when he strode into his Battle Creek Health Sanatorium clad in a coonskin hat and bearskin coat and gloves, while carrying in each hand an ornate Chinese lantern, he got more attention than he bargained for. Not recognizing him in his get-up, attendants figured he belonged in a different sort of sanatorium and promptly pitched their boss out the door.

That indignity somewhat soured the strong man on the "Cereal City," and he soon closed shop and shifted his muscle-building crusade to Chicago where he launched a "Healthatorium." But Battle Creek had not seen the last of "the bare torso king."

The "king" had started life anything but royal. He was born in 1868 on a hard-scrabble Missouri farm to a tubercular mother and abusive, alcoholic father. Bernard Adolphus McFadden they named him. When his father expired in a fit of delirium tremens, his mother sent her six-year-old sickly son to his aunt and uncle in Illinois. The youth's health grew worse, due largely to hateful treatment, overwork and little food. As he grew sicker, to avoid the cost of a funeral his miserable relatives bound him out as a farm laborer. But life on the farm saved his - he worked hard, ate all he wanted of wholesome food and gained weight and muscle

At the age of 12, he fled the farm, hopping a train to St. Louis where he eked out a livelihood through a series of odd jobs. His poor health returned, and doctors offered little hope. When he was 15, epiphany came in the unlikely guise of a gymnasium. An old wrestler befriended him and taught him the

Bernarr Macfadden, America's prototype muscle man,
tried to market his cereal, Strengtho, in Battle Creek.

ropes, so to speak. The youth took to constantly carrying around a ten-pound lump of lead. Not only was his health restored, but he rippled and bulged.

Three years after he had discovered the secret to perfect health through dumbbells and push-ups, he decided to share his knowledge with the world. Changing his first name to Bernarr, which he thought sounded like the roar of a lion, and altering the spelling of his last name to Macfadden, more masculine he felt, he hung out his shingle as "Bernarr Macfadden - Kinistherapist - Teacher of Higher Physical Culture." Few students responded but the muscle builder persevered, bouncing around between New York and Chicago, as he added new dimensions to his doctrine.

He invented exercise devices utilizing pulleys, ropes and springs. He developed workout routines for nearly every part of the body including the eyelids. To make hair stronger, he yanked on it throughout the day. For tougher teeth, he chewed chunks of wood - mahogany not pine. He also advocated vegetarianism, fresh air, sleeping on the floor, walking barefoot to absorb the earth's beneficial magnetism, air baths (strutting around naked), fasting as a panacea and grapes as a cancer cure. In 1899, he ventured into publishing with his magazine *Physical Culture*. Its masthead carried the motto "Weakness A Crime - Don't Be A Criminal." By World War I its circulation reached 500,000, and the strong man had become a rich man.

As Macfadden chinned himself out of poverty, Battle Creek gained national reputation for its health industry. It all began in 1863 when Seventh Day Adventist prophetess Ellen G. White experienced a vision during a visit to an Otsego farmhouse that spurred her followers to embrace vegetarianism. Subsequent visions put her church squarely in the campaign for health reform through water therapy, inside and out, plenty of graham crackers, as well as the avoidance of hard cider, coffee, tea, greasy food, pickles and tight corset lacing.

In 1866, the Adventists opened a health reform institute in Battle Creek. It limped along for a decade until the arrival of an energetic young superintendent named Dr. John Harvey Kellogg. The five-foot, three-inch dynamo dubbed the place the Battle Creek Sanitarium, energized the operation and by 1881 the "San" was well on its way to becoming a mecca for hundreds of thousands of well-heeled, run-down patients. In his spare time Dr. Kellogg invented health foods such as granola, caramel cereal coffee, peanut butter, and with his brother W.K. Kellogg's help, corn flakes.

Kellogg's food inventions failed to attract many consumers until C.W. Post, a salesman from Texas, checked into the San for several months, found the fare to his liking and in 1894 began marketing his own version of the coffee substitute which he named Postum. Thanks to his advertising genius, sales grew lustily. He followed that success with Grape Nuts, Post Toasties and other breakfast foods. By the turn-of-the-century Post had become a millionaire. Scores of breakfast entrepreneurs sought to emulate his success, and a Battle Creek cereal boom resulted. Ultimately, more than 100 cereal companies would call the city home.

Macfadden, never one to spurn a chance to disrobe and pose or a business opportunity, decided to muscle in on the Battle Creek bonanza with a double-barreled attack. In 1908, he rented a huge fieldstone structure that had been built a few years before for the Phelps Sanatorium, an ill-fated attempt to compete with Dr. Kellogg's San. Macfadden solicited patients to sample his bizarre health theories with a tough pitch: "If you have enough vitality to be alive, you have sufficient vital strength to develop at least a normal degree of health, and if you remain a weakling, you have no one to blame but yourself." But the main reason he wanted a Battle Creek site was to market his own breakfast cereal: Strengtho.

Unfortunately, Strengtho proved a bit too strong for the public's palate, chiefly because the wheat germ-based product turned rancid shortly after packaging. His Sanitarium, too, went belly-up soon after Macfadden got hurled into the snow by his employees. The fact that his milk and grape therapy for cancer patients brought little relief did not help matters.

But the Battle Creek debacle rankled Macfadden enough to make two more business attempts there. In 1921, he opened a sanatorium in a vacant community house at the edge of Camp Custer. It failed, and the following year he moved to a mansion on Maple Street where he conducted the International Health Resort Association. It remained in operation for two or three years, and then Macfadden quietly left Battle Creek for the last time.

Elsewhere, Macfadden continued to prosper via his publishing empire which ultimately encompassed 79 health books he wrote and scores of magazines such as *True Detective*, *True Story*, *True Romance*, *Photoplay* and *Liberty*. During the Depression he became a multimillionaire. But hubris in the form of political aspirations hastened his downfall. After he spent nearly a million dollars of his publishing corporation's funds attempting to enter the political arena, he was forced to resign as its president.

But even as his financial prowess weakened, he remained physically vital through exercise and diet. He married for the fourth time at the age of 80 and celebrated his 81st birthday by making a parachute jump. Macfadden died in 1955 at the age of 87, of jaundice aggravated by his attempt to cure the condition through fasting.

The monumental fieldstone structure where Macfadden conducted his first Battle Creek venture survived "the bare torso king" by 30 years. In 1911, Dr. Kellogg took over the building and used it as an annex to the San. When the U.S. Army acquired the main San in 1942 and converted it to Percy Jones Hospital, Kellogg moved his entire operation to the "Fieldstone San." Despite National Historic Register status and a hard-fought campaign by local preservationists, the magnificent structure fell victim to the wrecking ball in 1985.

The historic "Fieldstone San" where Macfadden first tried his
Battle Creek scheme was razed in 1985.

When A President's Morals Went On Trial

The packed courtroom hushed as the president took the stand to testify about intimate details of his private life while in the White House. Among the newspaper reporters, government officials, family members and secret service agents summoned as witnesses, as well as curious onlookers anxious to be part of the historic drama, sat many who recognized the charges brought against the former chief executive of the United States as a vindictive Republican ploy to sully his reputation.

Newspaper headlines proclaimed it the "trial of the century" when in 1913, ex-president Theodore Roosevelt battled in the Marquette County Courthouse to prove allegations that he was a drunkard nothing but politically motivated lies.

Born of a wealthy New York family in 1858, Roosevelt had overcome a sickly youth through athletics, then launched a frenetic career as an author, reform politician, cowboy, New York City police commissioner and cavalry hero of San Juan Hill. Elected vice-president in 1900, he assumed the presidency upon William McKinley's assassination the following year.

During two terms as president he brought new vigor to the office, advocating the strenuous life, accomplishing an aggressive foreign policy epitomized by "speak softly and carry a big stick," and promoting much-needed domestic reforms in interstate commerce, food and drug protection, conservation and regulation of big business. He relinquished office in 1909 to his friend, William H. Taft, but that portly president's conservative policies drove Roosevelt to vie for the Republican nomination in 1912. When Taft's control of party machinery won him renomination, Roosevelt supporters bolted to found the Progressive or "Bull Moose" party.

Because of his animated speaking style, Republican enemies branded Teddy Roosevelt a drunk.

The bitterly fought campaign, featuring much mud slinging, divided the Republican vote and made possible the election of Democrat Woodrow Wilson. Roosevelt, in particular, became the victim of scurrilous rumors that he drank heavily, based simply on his animated speaking style and ruddy-faced enthusiasm.

Michigan, a bastion of the Republican Party since its birth in Jackson in 1854, emerged as a hotly contested battleground in 1912. Beginning with shenanigans at the Republican State Convention in Bay City, the issue splintered the party, with business interests backing Taft and working class voters favoring their hero Roosevelt. The campaign turned particularly nasty in the western Upper Peninsula where mine owners bullied employees to remain regular Republicans but miners embraced the Bull Moose Party.

Roosevelt stumped through the Upper Peninsula in October 1912, and during a speech in Marquette vigorously promoted election of local Progressive candidates. Roosevelt's telling foray incensed staunchly conservative Republican George A. Newett, editor of the nearby Ishpeming *Iron Ore* mining journal. He dashed off a scathing editorial in his October 12 issue charging, "Roosevelt lies and curses in a most disgusting way, he gets drunk too, and that not infrequently, and all his intimates know about it."

While political enemies had bruited barbs about the president's excessive drinking since 1907, no established newspaper had dared give them credence. Roosevelt had publicly ignored the slurs, but out of a strong sense of duty to defend his honor he decided "that on the first occasion when they were published by a paper of sufficient standing to warrant my taking action, I would do so." Roosevelt investigated the *Iron Ore* and found it an established weekly of approximately 4,000 circulation. Two weeks after Newett's editorial, he ordered his attorneys to commence a libel suit.

In the November 1912 election, Roosevelt and running mate Hiram Johnson of California swept Michigan by a plurality of 62,340 votes. Progressive candidates also scored resounding victories in Marquette County. Consequently, many figured Roosevelt would drop his charges against Newett after the election. But the old Rough Rider had the bit in his teeth and determined to scotch the tosspot rap once and for all.

As the May 26, 1913 trial date drew near, Marquette buzzed with excitement. Most of the city's working class citizens sided with Roosevelt, believing he did not drink to excess or if he did, given his spectacular career, it did not matter to them. Some 200 cheering townspeople greeted the former president when he arrived at the Northwestern Railroad depot early on the morning of the trial. A retinue of 25 character witnesses, powerful and nationally respected men in their own right, accompanied him.

The trial began that afternoon, with Judge Richard C. Flannigan presiding. So many spectators sought entrance to the big sandstone Marquette County Courthouse that Sheriff James Moloney cordoned off the doors, allowing in only those with special passes. But some locals managed to circumvent the sheriff. A pair of teen-aged girls slid down an unguarded coal shute and, despite blackened bottoms, enjoyed a day of the trial.

The first order of business, to choose twelve unprejudiced jurors, proved a challenge. Flannigan buttressed the normal pool of 36 with 50 additional veniremen. Roosevelt's and Newett's attorneys scratched outspoken Republicans and Progressives. One venireman who insisted he was impartial arrived in court sporting a huge Bull Moose pin. A big ham fisted Irishman claimed to be objective, but when the court learned he had been thrashing anyone he encountered who spoke against Roosevelt he was excused. After 45 veniremen had been interviewed, twelve jurors, mostly farmers, teamsters and miners, were selected. To insure they remained unbiased, Flannigan ordered them to sleep on cots under guard in the courthouse for the duration of the trial.

The rival attorneys jockeyed the judge to have their opponents testify first. Flannigan ruled for Newett: Roosevelt would take the stand to deny the charges, followed by his character witnesses. Newett and the 40 witnesses he claimed had observed the president drunk would have the final say.

Roosevelt began his testimony on Tuesday morning. He spoke in a "precise, slow and decisive voice, in which he articulated every syllable separately and with great distinctness" as he vehemently denied Newett's allegations. Swearing that he had never been intoxicated and that he detested the taste of alcoholic beverages, he itemized practically every time in his life that he had taken a drink.

"I do not smoke and I do not drink beer and I don't drink red wine," he testified. "I have never drunk whiskey or brandy except when the doctor prescribed it, or possibly on some occasion after great exposure when I was chilled through." During his entire eleven-month-long African hunting tour he had taken but "seven tablespoons of brandy." Not a total abstainer, he did admit enjoying a glass or two of white wine with dinner, a glass of champagne once a month and, while in the White House, "a half dozen mint-juleps a year but only one at a time."

A solid hour of cunning cross examination by Newett's lead attorney failed to discredit a word of Roosevelt's testimony. Then, during the reminder of the week, 35 witnesses corroborated Roosevelt's activities during almost every hour of his waking life for the previous 15 years. Social worker and long time friend Jacob Riis called the allegations "monstrous lies!" His family physician, Dr. Alexander Lambert, and former U.S. Navy Surgeon General, Dr. Presley Rixley, told the court Roosevelt was a temperate man, "as moderate as a man could be without being a teetotaler." Other nationally prominent witnesses, including ex-Secretary of the Navy Truman Newberry, former cabinet officials James R. Garfield and George B. Cortelyou, forester Gifford Pinchot, and fellow Spanish American War veterans Adm. George Dewey and Maj. Gen. Leonard Wood, swore under oath as to the ex-president's sober nature.

Then came newspaper correspondents, including some who had been assigned to keep a close watch on his drinking habits during the 1912 election, cousins from Oyster Bay, naturalists who had traveled with him in Africa, household servants and secret service agents who had guarded him while president to completely refute Newett's allegations.

Throughout the week, Newett's attorneys continued a show of confidence, stating they would "fight as long as there is a foot to stand on." Press leaks revealed their strategy to produce witnesses who had seen Roosevelt "with a snoutful," who had been present while he delivered a speech in Duluth "three sheets to the wind" and who had heard the ex-president respond to the question, "Will you have a little drink with me?" during House Speaker "Uncle Joe" Cannon's birthday party with, "No, I will have a big drink with you."

When Roosevelt's last witness finished on Saturday morning, Newett walked "with quick and springing steps to the stand." Facing the jury, he pulled four typed sheets from his pocket and read his statement. After an extensive nationwide search for evidence, he had been unable to locate a single witness who would swear that he had actually seen Roosevelt drink to excess. Profoundly impressed by the enormous weight of evidence Roosevelt had mustered, Newett was now "forced to the conclusion I was mistaken."

"Good, bully, that's just what I wanted; that settles it!" roared Roosevelt. Receiving permission to address the entire court, Roosevelt rose and asked the jury to award only nominal damages, as he had not entered the suit for money but merely to exonerate his reputation.

The jury soon returned a verdict for Roosevelt, who under Michigan law could have been awarded $10,000. But Newett was assessed the minimum - six cents in damages, "the price of a good newspaper." Headlines across the nation hailed the verdict. Roosevelt had vindicated his good name and henceforth no serious historian would question his sobriety.

Eighty-five years later, even as another president attempted to fend off litigation concerning his morals, an official State of Michigan historical marker on the Marquette Courthouse square continued to commemorate the landmark case when Teddy Roosevelt brought a big stick to the U.P. and won back his honor.

Constructed in 1902-1904, the Marquette County Court house was the scene of Roosevelt's 1913 libel trial.

209

"There Is No Such Thing As A Bad Boy"

A trinity of memories bounded the ragamuffin's world. Indelible remained the image of the sheet pulled over his mother's pallid face. Then, one day his father locked Louis alone in their hotel room as he left carrying his baby sister. He returned without her. Not long after, his father took the six-year-old to downtown Detroit to view Christmas decorations. Enraptured by grand windows displays, the Christ child and Santa Claus, angels and toy trains, he did not notice his father had released his hand. And when he turned, he was gone, forever.

Next came a nightmare blur of strange uncaring faces as he ran in terror, tears streaming down his cheeks. He scavenged for food behind restaurants and in trash cans. He slept huddled with other street arabs in hallways or over iron gratings, from which drifted up the smell of baking in the basement. Finally, a policemen collared him. Lodged with the Society for the Prevention of Cruelty to Children and placed in one unhappy home after another, he grew hard. He repeatedly ran away. He learned to steal, to fight, to survive on the cruel streets. Labeled a "bad boy," he wound up in the Detroit Detention Home.

Then one day, the skinny little waif found himself aboard a Michigan Central train bound for an experimental rehabilitation program that had been launched just two months before. When the engine chugged to a stop at the Albion depot, a tall thin man, 30-years-old, neatly dressed in a suit and tie, awaited. Taking the boy by the hand, he introduced himself as Floyd Starr, and then asked, "Who is there, Louis, I wonder, who loves you?" With big, sad, brown eyes the youth looked up at Starr for a long time before he answered: "Well, I guess there ain't nobody - 'cept maybe just God."

Starr could empathize. Born in 1883 on a farm near Decatur, he had experienced an unhappy childhood, receiving little love from his improvident father, his mother who had already borne four children and did not really want another or his much older siblings. But "as the twig is bent so grows the tree," and at the age of four came an event that planted the seeds for Starr's life work. During a Sunday evening get-together, the boy overheard a conversation about a man who had adopted 50 children. Asking his mother what adopt meant, she answered, "Some children don't have a mama or a papa, so a nice man takes them into his own home." Starr replied, "Well when I get big, I'm going to buy a farm and adopt 50 children to live on it."

That childhood vision remained crystal clear as the family moved to Benton Harbor, then to a farm five miles southwest of Marshall. Starr attended Marshall High School where he excelled in oratory and graduated as class president in 1902. He took to the road as a lecturer for the WCTU, studied for a semester at Kalamazoo College, then came under the sway of Bernarr Macfadden, health-through-fitness guru, and Dr. John Harvey Kellogg, colorful proprietor of the world-famous wellness spa, the Battle Creek Sanitarium. Kellogg, who Starr learned was the man who adopted 50 children he had heard about as a four-year-old, became an important influence in his development. Kellogg urged him to return to school, and in 1907 Starr enrolled in Albion College where he graduated three years later.

In 1910, Starr married his college sweetheart, Harriet Armstrong. They moved to Chicago where both worked at Macfadden's Healthatorium. But the desire to work with boys continued strong, and in 1912 the couple secured positions with the Beulah Land Farm for Boys, a "life saving station for homeless boys" near Boyne City. Starr's elation at finally working in the field of his dreams soon turned sour when the farm's director, Herman Swift, was arrested and convicted of "taking liberties with young boys." Starr supervised the closing of the institute and placement of as many of the boys as he could.

He resolved to start his own operation, and in 1913 Starr plowed his entire life savings of $1,900 into a rocky, run-down 40-acre farm bordering Montcalm Lake, three miles east of Albion. The only buildings still standing were an old barn and a rickety sheep shed. He began building a cottage on the foundation of the old farmhouse that had burned years prior. Before the structure Starr named Gladsome Cottage could be completed, two boys from the Beulah Farm drifted in like stray dogs. October 3, 1913, when the cottage stood ready, thirteen boys already called the farm home. By the year's end nine more arrived, sent by progressive judges and social workers desperately seeking something better than institutionalization for juvenile offenders and orphans.

The articles of association of The Starr Commonwealth For Boys cited its purpose as "the maintenance and operation of homes for vagrant and friendless boys and for the instruction of such boys in the various mechanical trades and other vocations of life." But the real philosophy behind Starr's avant-garde academy lay in the creed he drafted one evening in Gladsome Cottage:

We believe that there is no such thing as a bad boy. We believe that badness is not a normal condition but it is the result of misdirected energy. We believe that every normal boy will be good if given an opportunity in an environment of love and activity. We believe in the dignity of labor. We believe that each child should be given some work suitable to childhood and that he could be taught that the value of labor is to be found, not alone in the com-

pleted tasks, but in the training of the mind and the hand, and in the joy of accomplishment. We believe also in play. Play is the child's normal means of self-expression...

At the Commonwealth, under Starr's guidance the boys governed themselves through committees and voting. They studied part of the day and worked the farm and played the remainder. Chores ranging from milking cows, gardening, cooking and washing dishes became an integral part of the curriculum. Starr also made sure his charges were exposed to fine literature, music, art and other cultural endeavors. But above all else, the man who came to be known by all as Uncle Floyd gave the boys a sense of family and love.

Little Louis arrived at the Commonwealth in late November 1913. His papers read "history

The camera captured "Uncle" Floyd reading to his boys, ca. 1914.

unknown." Even his birth date was a mystery. Starr and the boys voted Louis a birthday, the same as Abraham Lincoln's, February 12. On that day came a cake with nine candles, the first such celebration he had known. The friendship, love, counsel and understanding Louis found in his new home soon transformed him from an "incorrigible young hoodlum" to a sweet little boy.

He had been there about two weeks when he asked, "Uncle Floyd, may I go without my meal today? "Aren't you hungry, Louis?" he questioned. "Yes, I'm hungry, but in Detroit I know a lot of kids that are hungry just as I was; they don't have the nice food that we have. If you let me go without my meal and give me the price of my meal, I'd like to send it to a lady in Detroit that I know and she would buy a meal for some poor kid."

Deeply moved, Starr told him to eat his meal, and afterwards see if any of the other boys wanted to participate in the plan. At dinner a beaming Louis announced: "Oh, yes, Uncle Floyd, I asked the boys. We all want to do it. We all want to give our dinner to those other kids." And thus began the tradition called Fast Day.

Starr's devotion to his boys during the tough early days of the Commonwealth, the struggle to make ends meet when each week saw more hungry little faces crowd the dinner table, took its toll. Unable to cope, Harriet left with their two children and secured a divorce.

But things gradually improved as Starr campaigned far and near for donations. Teachers, counselors and other staff members joined the team. The campus grew by leaps and bounds, swallowing up neighboring farms, and dozens of new structures - residences for boys, a dining complex, a schoolhouse, a gym, a chapel and a museum dotted the immaculately groomed grounds.

In 1914, the Commonwealth began selling unique Christmas seals that for decades brought much-needed funding. The following year, Uncle Floyd's family had grown to his childhood dream size - 50 boys. In 1920, the 100th boy graduated from the Commonwealth. Twenty-five years later, the graduates numbered 1,000, including 400 who served in the armed forces during World War II.

Over the decades Starr's work attracted famous authors, artists, screen celebrities and statesmen. In the early days, poets Rabindranath Tagore and Kahil Gibran became devotees. The 1930s and 1940s brought repeated visits by Helen Keller, George Washington Carver, Carl Sandburg and Jesse Stuart. Later, Roy Rogers and Dale Evans, Art Linkletter, Eddie Arnold and Joan Crawford lent their support to the Commonwealth.

Starr retired from active leadership in 1967, to be succeeded by Larry Bentro and Arlin Ness. He continued to provide valuable guidance until his death at the age of 97 in 1980. The institution he started on a shoestring and a dream in 1913 continues its vital work in salvaging the lives of boys and, at its adjunct campuses in Ohio, of girls.

Louis Bernard, the Detroit urchin with a heart of gold, became one of only three of his boys Starr allowed to call him "Dad." Louis carved out a successful career with a New York importing firm and raised a fine family of seven, including his oldest son named Floyd.

And each December, everyone at Starr Commonwealth, boys, staff and guests, still voluntarily go without dinner on Fast Day, so that its cost can be sent to destitute children even less fortunate than they.

Stogie Stories

One of four daughters born to poor Polish immigrants, she started her working life as a stripper when but 14-years-old. Small for her age and with two long braids down her back, she was not very good at first. At the end of her initial week's work of six nine-hour days, her Detroit employer handed her a pay envelope containing 23 cents. With practice, she grew more skillful. By the month's end she was making $2 per week.

Some days the boss put her to "booking" or used her as a "side worker." The hours were long and the intense tobacco smell made her head ache, but she persevered. Her older sister had made it as a "roller." Another sibling was a well paid "buncher." Besides, it was not like she planned to spend her whole life doing this - someday she hoped to marry and start a family of her own. By 1914 she and her three sisters in the trade were bringing home weekly pay envelopes containing $19, $14, $13 and $12. With daughters so profitable, their father retired from work that year.

Such was life in the Michigan cigar industry as documented by a 1914 legislative investigation. It was an era when real men smoked stogies - none of those sissified little paper tubes the French called cigarettes. And in huge city factories and small town "buckeye" operations across the peninsulas, Michigan cigar makers answered the national demand by producing hundreds of millions of the large brown rolls annually.

Tobacco, a gift of the new world, was used in the form of pipes, snuff, chew, cigars and cigarettes by the Americas' indigenous peoples. Archeological evidence suggests the Mayans invented the cigar. Fifteenth and sixteenth century European explorers noted its use among numerous cultures. Lionel Wafer, who toured Central America in 1699, reported the use of cigars "as thick as a man's wrist and two or three feet in length." Those baseball bat-sized cigars served communal duty - one person puffed his mightest and several hundred natives greedily snuffed up the secondhand smoke.

But, with the exception of Spain and its possessions, cigar smoking long took a back seat to pipes, snuff and "chaw." During the first decades of the 19th-century, stogies began their climb to popularity in America. The first American cigar factory went into production in the Connecticut River Valley in 1810. President John Quincy Adams, a connoisseur of Havana cigars, brought respectability to puffing them during the 1820s. So many Bostonians followed his example that city fathers passed a law restricting cigar smokers to a section of Boston Commons. Following the Civil War, popular President Ulysses S. Grant helped inspire a national rage for cheroots. His death of throat cancer in 1885 failed to stem the tide. The cigar emerged as the dominant American nicotine delivery system.

Manufacturers grew by leaps and bounds to keep pace with the national addiction. It took little capital to go into business; all that was needed was a supply of tobacco, a table, a few simple tools and the requisite skill.

By 1870 cigar making had gained a foothold in Michigan's economy. That year the U.S. census taker found two pioneer cigar factories in Kalamazoo. Lilienfeld Brothers and Kepler & Company employed 31 men to hand-roll over a million cigars annually. The Lilienfeld family opened a branch factory in Detroit the following year to produce its popular "Lilies" cigar. By 1874, 1,600 Michiganders worked in tobacco and cigar factories. Thirty years later, Michigan boasted 525 cigar manufacturers ranging from bustling factories to mom and pop home-based operations. Sixty-eight of the state's 83 counties claimed at least one cigar factory. But over 50% of Michigan's annual output of 231 million cigars came from Wayne County. Kalamazoo County tied with Houghton County for second place in the cigar sweepstakes.

While Detroit's Wayne Cigar Co. and San Telmo Cigar Co. each employed over a thousand workers, it was a rare community during the first decade of the 20th century that lacked its homegrown cigar maker. In Plainwell, M.W. Estes employed three rollers. Beginning in 1908, Paw Paw's L.E. Griffith operated a four-man cigar company. South Haven had Klock & Sherwood and former sailor Evert S. Dyckman's firm.

In 1904, 15 Kalamazoo firms rolled 16 million cigars. The Lilienfeld and Verdon cigar companies employed large work forces. Smaller concerns included the Kalamazoo Cigar Co., which offered "Charles Darwin" cigars for a nickel each, The Bell Cigar Co. and John Gemrich.

Handsomely-made wooden cigar boxes, decorated with finely-printed art work and distinctive brand

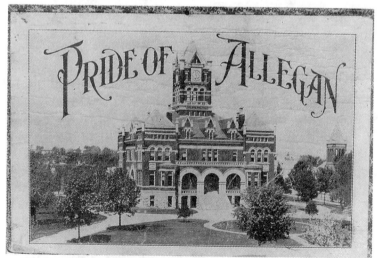

The Carl Cigar Co. marketed its hand-rolled stogies in boxes depicted Allegan's pride, the magnificent courthouse that fell victim to the wrecking ball in 1961.

names, proved a popular advertising technique. Beginning in 1881, Kalamazoo's Elias Goldberg packed his "Little Beauty" cigars in a box that pictured gamboling children. F.E. McClannon's "Miss Kazoo" brand featured a buxom, Gibsonesque, young miss. Charles Holt appealed to more political-minded smokers with his "United States Senator," which depicted the bearded visage of Kalamazoo's powerful Republican senator, Julius Caesar Burrows.

A Saginaw cigar maker marketed his wares to sportsmen smokers. At the angler's feet lay dual piles of fish and stogies.

In 1903, Allegan's Carl Cigar Co. began rolling "Pride of Allegan" cigars. Each box featured the facade of the city's majestic Romanesque courthouse that unfortunately fell victim to the wrecking ball in 1961. The Ben King Cigar Co. of St. Joseph employed 11 workers to produce cigars bearing the likeness of that lamented local poet. The Mertz Cigar Co. in Saginaw made a pitch to sportsmen with its "Speckled Sports" cigars that came in boxes illustrated with a contented trout fisherman. Who the Holland based Snag Cigar Co. was appealing to with its motto, "If you

219

want a good smoke go and get a Snag," is open to conjecture. And a century before "Joe Camel" targeted children, Detroit's Brown Brothers proffered "Newsboy" cigars with a lithograph of young Detroit *Free Press* carriers playing cards and smoking cigars.

Plenty of youngsters also found employment in turn-of-the century cigar factories. In 1904, Michigan inspectors identified 560 children under the age of 16 working full time in cigar factories at an average daily wage of 57 cents.

Cigar making traditionally had been a trade monopolized by males. But by 1914 Michigan women had almost completely supplanted men as cigar factory workers. Especially in the huge Detroit factories, most workers were the daughters of Polish and German immigrants.

Because it was a trade that demanded considerable training, employers preferred hiring 14-year-old girls as apprentices. If the girls stayed seven or eight years in the factory before quitting to marry and become homemakers, the management could easily recoup the year's training it took before they were working at full speed.

The craft consisted of highly specialized tasks. Strippers, the least skilled class, tore out the mid rib of the tobacco leaf. Selectors sorted the leaves by color and size and "booked" them into bundles. Bunchers bound the loose filler into a binder leaf in the palm of their hands or more commonly pressed out the embryonic cigars in wooden molds. Rollers cut the prized outside wrapper to the exact size, carefully rolled it around the bunch, shaped and rounded off the head, sealed it with a swipe of licorice-flavored paste and trimmed off any stray ends. As a final stamp of approval they often nipped off the cigar's end with nicotine stained teeth.

Highly paid packers selected similar sized cigars, picked the best for the top row and carefully fit them into boxes of 50. Finally, banders unboxed the cigars, placed colorful brand bands around each and repacked them. Young girls just starting out in the trade often got detailed as side workers to carry supplies to the craftsmen.

Cigar makers were paid a piece rate and earned salaries commensurate with their speed, skill and the difficulty of their particular specialty. In 1914, most skilled cigar makers earned from $7 to $20 for a six-day work week, at a time when more than 50% of Michigan's women workers earned less than $8 per week. Cigar makers had achieved their high wage scale largely because the industry had become heavily unionized following the Civil War.

But union activity proved the downfall of Kalamazoo's major cigar factories. Following a tense labor dispute in 1908, the Lilies Cigar Co. shifted its entire operation to Detroit with its more manageable immigrant labor pool. The following year, the Verdon Factory closed as well. Its brick building, still standing on Willard Street, later housed the Bowers Lighter Co.

Some of the big factories' workers stayed in Kalamazoo and launched their own businesses. The 1910 *Kalamazoo City Directory* lists 24 cigar making firms. The last of the breed in Kalamazoo, John Vander Weele, hand rolled his final stogie in 1968.

As the twentieth century wore on, cigar making in Michigan became a forgotten art as cigars lost increasing ground to cigarettes, romanticized by Hollywood and embraced by female smokers. As southern cigarette factories grew by leaps and bounds, entrepreneurs discovered a novel use for the tobacco dust generated in the manufacturing process: it became a highly sought after agricultural pesticide. And interestingly enough, scientific studies in the 1920s demonstrated that the dust's insect-killing power was in direct relationship to its nicotine content.

When Billy Sunday
Slid Into Detroit

Twenty-nine thousand Detroit working men squeezed into the huge tabernacle built to hold 16,000 on a September Sabbath in 1916. They had come to hear the Rev. Billy Sunday, the most flamboyant, outspoken and popular evangelist America had yet spawned. And that day the bible beater was hot, hotter than a two dollar pistol.

The old baseball player raced across the stage and like a sinner trying to slide into heaven executed as sweet a hook slide into home as ever seen at the Tigers' Navin Field. He pounded on the floor, he jumped on a chair, he shook his fist at the "real, genuine, blazing-eyed, cloven-hoofed, forked-tail, old devil." He leaped high in the air to catch an imaginary fly ball. He worked himself into such a sweat that he shed his coat, tie and vest to demonstrate the difference between a fighting Christian and a "hog-jowled, weasel-eyed, sponge-columned, mushy-fisted, jelly-spined, pussy-footing, four-flushing, charlotte-russe Christian."

He caught his breath as the 5,000-member choir led the audience in singing "Rock of Ages," "Bringing in the Sheaves" and Michigan's own "The Old Rugged Cross." Then he wound up and let fly a "spit ball right into the devil's teeth." He railed against smoking, chewing, dancing and card playing. But he saved his special spleen for the liquor traffic, hollering: "As long as I have a foot I'll kick it; as long as I have a fist I'll hit it; as long as I have a tooth I'll bite it; as long as I have a head I'll butt it; and when I'm old and gray and bootless and toothless I'll gum it until I get to heaven and it goes to hell."

And when he was finished, a torrent of sinners filed down the "sawdust trail" to shake the preacher's hand and take the pledge to renounce cigarettes and saloons, poker playing and polka dancing.

Billy Sunday in action, ca. 1916.

The man who had dedicated his life to taunting others into "getting right with God" had himself seen the light 29 years before. Prior to that he been no stranger to the fun things he now proclaimed so evil.

Born in 1862 in a log cabin near Ames, Iowa, and named for his father, a Civil War soldier who did not survive to see his son, William Ashley Sunday endured a poverty-stricken childhood on a windswept frontier farm. He later told audiences, "I am a rube of the rubes. I am a hayseed of the hayseeds, and the malodors of the barnyard are on me yet." Unable to make ends meet any longer, his mother sent Billy at the age of 12 to the Soldiers Orphanage at Glenwood, Iowa. Two years later, he struck out on his own, working as hotel porter, janitor and stable boy while attending high school.

He shifted to Marshalltown, Iowa, where his job as an undertaker's assistant left enough spare time to join the prestigious fire brigade, with his primary duty to run foot races in the numerous tournaments the firemen waged. A natural athlete, he could run like the wind. He also joined the local baseball team, and with him playing outfield the Marshalltown nine won the state championship in 1883. His running and fielding skills caught the eye of the legendary Cap Anson, who signed him on with his Chicago White Stockings.

Never too hot a hitter, big league pitchers struck him out his first 13 times at bat. But when he did get on base he was a terror. He became the first player to circle the diamond in 14 seconds, and one season he stole 95 bases, a record broken only by Ty Cobb in 1915.

Fans loved his base-running bravado, his daring slides and gravity defying catches. Fellow players embraced their affable young teammate, always ready with a joke and a grin and a round for the house in the neighborhood bars the team called home when not on the field.

One Sunday afternoon in 1887, he and the boys got tanked up in a Chicago saloon, stumbled out into the daylight and with heads spinning slumped to the curb at the corner of State and Madison streets. Across the road a company of evangelists blew horns, flutes and slide trombones and sang the familiar old gospel hymns he remembered from his Iowa boyhood. Tears streaming down his cheeks, Sunday left his comrades sitting on the curb, followed the evangelists to the Pacific Garden Mission and "staggered out of sin and into the arms of the Savior."

The convert abandoned his low-down ways and joined the Jefferson Park Presbyterian Church. There, he met and wooed Helen Thompson, daughter of a Scottish ice cream manufacturer. The dour Scot was not pleased at the prospect of a baseball player as a son-in-law, but Sunday gradually won him over as he worked his way up the hierarchy of church work. He married Helen in 1888.

By then, Sunday had become increasingly passionate about his new-found religion, pushing its tenets on team mates, upbraiding those who chewed, cussed, guzzled, gambled or gamboled. He also refused to play ball on the Sabbath. Perhaps for that reason, Anson traded the young zealot to Pittsburgh. A year later he found himself a player for Philadelphia, where after eight seasons in the big leagues Sunday decided he could not "serve two masters." Turning down a $3,500 per year contract with Philadelphia, major money in those days, he took a job with the Chicago YMCA.

Gradually moving into more active soul-saving, Sunday held his first revival meeting in Garner, Iowa, in 1896. He honed his unique style during a decade of preaching in small Iowa towns, and his reputation grew by leaps and bounds. Then he stormed big cities across the nation, filling specially built big tabernacles with middle class audiences thirsty for salvation.

Ultimately he spoke to more than 100 million people and reputedly converted one million. By 1914 a national poll ranked him eighth as the "greatest man in the United States."

In the fall of 1916, Sunday set his sights on the burgeoning "Motor City" where, he concluded, "God, You've got a job on your hands in Detroit." In early December, his Detroit sponsors completed construction of a colossal tabernacle at the old Detroit Athletic Club grounds between Woodward and Cass avenues, "the largest auditorium for an exclusively religious purpose ever built in America."

The evangelist arrived at Detroit's Michigan Central Train Depot on September 9. An enormous crowd, larger than had greeted President Woodrow Wilson but months before, elbowed and jostled to catch a glimpse of the nattily dressed "sky pilot." Automobile magnate Henry M. Leland gave Sunday one of his new $8,000 Cadillac limousines in which the minister drove to department store tycoon S.S. Kresge's mansion, where he and staff lived luxuriously during their eight-week stay.

During his first three services on September 10, he let 44,000 Detroiters "have it right between the eyes." He bellowed: "An angel from heaven could not live in Detroit a week and keep company with the people you loaf with and get back into heaven without being purified with carbolic acid and formaldehyde." Being told of their depravity only increased Sunday's following. The Detroit *Times*, which billed itself as "Michigan's Cleanest Newspaper," began printing the previous day's sermons verbatim in each issue.

Beyond his announced goal to convert 50,000, Sunday had another agenda in Detroit: to buoy the ongoing drive to prohibit alcohol, an issue to be decided by a state referendum vote on November 7, 1916. Sunday told his audiences, "Four-fifths of crime is due to poverty and all the poverty to whiskey." Whipping himself into a frenzy against the "rum-mongers," he would level his finger at some unfortunate tosspot in the crowd and roar that the man who drank was a "dirty, low-down, whiskey-soaked, beer-guzzling, bull-necked, foul-mouthed hypocrite."

Detroit's brewers, barkeeps and other "anti-drys" fought back, denouncing Sunday's appeal as "emotional insanity" that would lead to a "spiritual jag, to be followed by the inevitable dark brown taste of the morning after religious intoxication." Their rhetoric paled beside the preacher's rejoinder, "I'll fight that dirty, hog-jowled, booze gang until hell freezes over, then I'll buy skates and tackle them on the ice."

Following Sunday's visit with Henry Ford at his Highland Park plant, the inventor of the Model T and the five-dollar-a-day job jumped into the melee.

**As portrayed in this cartoon from 1916,
Sunday pulled no punches in denouncing alcohol**

Announcing that he had devoted a year to the study of denatured alcohol as a substitute for gasoline, Ford predicted that if Michigan voted for prohibition the state's breweries could be converted to production of a "cleaner, nicer, better fuel."

In October, Sunday addressed a crowd of 11,000 in Ann Arbor. After he had lambasted the liquor interests, a poll of University of Michigan students showed they favored prohibition seven to one. The evangelist wound up his Detroit crusade on November 5, when he preached to 50,000 people. Prior to collecting a "free will offering" of $50,000 - "come on, this is a tabernacle, not a taber-nickle" - he asked who would vote for prohibition and 10,000 stood up. The following day, during his last performance in Michigan, he traveled to Grand Rapids where 7,000 men rose to the same question.

On November 7, 1916, Michigan voters cast 353,378 votes for prohibition and 284,754 against. Thanks in no small part to Sunday's theatrics, those Michiganders who craved a drink soon had to resort to organized crime's bootleg booze.

But Sunday, with his hell-fire and brimstone emphasis on divine wrath rather than divine love and his denouncement of scientists and liberals, "which did much to intensify the prejudices of plain people against higher education," found himself out of step with the national mood of the 1920s. His audiences grew smaller, the offerings less generous. Yet he continued to battle "old split-hoof" until his death of a heart attack following a sermon in 1935 - two years after the 21st Amendment ended what few but teetotalers remembered as the "noble experiment."

Father Patrick Dunigan: Fighting Chaplain

The doughboys of the 126th Infantry, 32nd Division, coupled long gleaming bayonets to their heavy 30/06 Springfield rifles, chambered rounds and waited with pounding hearts for the signal to attack. It was 7 a.m. on August 28, 1918, along the Soissons Front some 50 miles northeast of Paris, France. For 15 long minutes, the Michigan soldiers pressed against the cold clay walls of the trench, waiting for the thunder of the promised Allied artillery barrage to soften up the German machine gun emplacements to their front. But the big guns never roared.

Nevertheless, at 7:15 Kalamazoo's Col. Joseph Westnedge ordered the advance to begin. Over the top, into the machine gun-raked, pock-marked no man's land they raced - into the shrieking shrapnel, barbed wire windrows and swirls of lung searing mustard gas. And over the top with "his boys," non combatant's arm brassard pulled off and a big 45 automatic thrust into his belt, scrambled Father "Pat" Dunigan, the "fighting priest" from Flint.

The ensuing five day battle for Juvigny, a desperate attack by the 10th French Army to which the 32nd Division had been attached, would witness the Americans overrun heavily entrenched German divisions and repulse a counter attack. Their heroism would earn them the nickname, "Les Terribles." Father Pat's exploits during that battle would also help establish his reputation as the "universally beloved chaplain who served with the American Expeditionary Force in the World War."

Without regard to his own safety, Dunigan was offering aid to the wounded when a spinning shard of shrapnel slammed into his helmet. He awoke with a throbbing head in a nearby cave that had been converted to a medical aid station. The medical officer in charge, Capt. Leo Crum of Kalamazoo, dressed Dunigan's severe head wound and told the priest to remain still because of the danger of exertion following such an injury. Then he returned to his grim duties as more and more stretchers filled with badly wounded soldiers littered the cave floor.

Suddenly, Dunigan appeared at his side, white and wan from his injury, but still insisting, against the doctor's advice, to help care for his "boys." Together they labored for some time until, feeling giddy, Dunigan stepped outside the cave to get some fresh air. Stretcher bearers found him there where he had blacked out. They quickly loaded him into an ambulance headed for a field hospital behind the front lines, placing Dunigan, a big heavy man, in a bottom rack and three other badly wounded soldiers at his side and above him. Shortly after the ambulance started for the hospital, a shell burst nearby, sending razor sharp sharpnel crashing into the vehicle. The soldier above the priest was struck and killed instantly. As his blood dripped down upon the lips of the chaplain below, it seemed to Dunigan to be fresh warm milk. And that was the last he remembered.

He regained consciousness hours later. Stiff and sore, and without clothes, he found himself in the mud by the side of the road. A dead man lay across his knees. He was so weak that it took a great exertion to roll the body off his legs.

After the shell explosion rocked the ambulance, the driver had checked on his patients. He found three dead, and Dunigan appeared lifeless as well. Following standing orders, the driver had dumped the bodies alongside the road and returned to the cave for another load of live patients.

After rolling the dead soldier off his legs, Dunigan staggered to his feet and got his bearings. He salvaged a uniform from a fallen soldier who lay nearby. The trousers were too small so he slit the side seams

**Father Dunigan (left) confers with Knights of Columbus
Director Fred Milan in 1918.**

and threaded them together with shoe laces.

That is how they found the chaplain, trudging up the road, not toward the hospital, but back to the front lines where he knew his place was with his boys of the 126th Infantry.

The fighting priest had been born July 15, 1871, in the St. Clair County community of Emmett, aptly named, although mispelled, by the Irish pioneers who settled there after Robert Emmet, the champion of Irish independence who was hanged by the British in 1803. Dunigan's grandfather was among the original settlers in the township, and his father Michael had been the first white child born there. Dunigan's deeply religious parents taught their four sons and two daughters to know right from wrong. And as part of their Celtic heritage, the Dunigan boys learned to back up their convictions with fists, if necessary.

Dunigan, a farm boy and naive to the ways of the world, took his first excursion away from home at the age of 15: a train ride to Imlay City, about 15 miles to the west. He was settled in his seat, enjoying in wide-eyed wonderment the passing scenery, when a "news butcher" passed down the aisle, hawking newspapers, magazines and racy paperback novels. His sales technique was to hand male passengers one of the paperbacks open to a particularly erotic passage and return several minutes later hoping they had become immersed in the story and would purchase the book.

The smut peddlar placed an open paperback in young Dunigan's lap. When he returned, the boy was waiting for him. Leaping to his feet, his blue eyes blazing in anger, he asked, "You put this book in my lap! Did you expect me to read it?

"Sure I did," responded the hawker, but whatever else he was about to say was silenced by the sharp crack of a hard right to the jaw. And the young slugger continued a volley of blows until the much bigger man "measured his length in the aisle."

Like many another Irish youth of that era, Dunigan might have parlayed his fistic prowess into a ring career, but by then he had already determined to study for the priesthood. When he was 18, he entered Assumption College in Sandwich, Ontario. Five years later, he transferred to St. Jerome's College in Kitchener for one year, and in 1898 he received his degree from St. Mary's Seminary in Baltimore, Maryland. The Rt. Rev. John S. Foley ordained him a priest that same year in Detroit. Dunigan first served as assistant pastor at St. Vincent's Parish in Detroit and then was appointed to pastorates in the rural communities of Argyle and Croswell in Sanilac County. By 1907 he had been transferred to the larger parish of Lapeer.

In 1910, a smallpox epidemic ravaged Lapeer, killing scores. The terror stricken citizens huddled in their houses while local doctors, nurses and undertakers struggled to meet the demand for their services. Dunigan visited grief stricken homes, caring for the sick, conforting the bereaved and burying the dead. His selfless services earned him a medal for heroism from the state of Michigan.

Two years later, local Republicans nominated him to run for mayor. During an era when a candidate's religion was of major concern and in a city with a Catholic population of only four percent, he won election by an overwhelming majority. He became one of the first Catholic priests to serve as mayor of an American city.

In Lapeer, Dunigan got interested in the Michigan National Guard. His friend and mentor, Father Francis C. Kelly of Lapeer, had served as chaplain of the Michigan troops during the Spanish American War. In 1907, Kelly asked Perley L. Abbey, prominent Kalamazoo drug manufacturer and colonel of the regiment then known as the 2nd Infantry, if he could be allowed to appoint his successor. Abbey seemed reluctant to grant that concession until Kelly told him he had Dunigan in mind. "That is altogether different; he is appointed," Abbey responded.

In the summer of 1913, Dunigan traveled to the Upper Peninsula copper country, as chaplain to the more than 2,500 National Guardmen dispatched there to police the violent copper miners' strike. Three years later, the entire Michigan National Guard, redesignated the 32nd Infantry, was mustered into federal service for duty on the Mexican border as part of the expedition led by Gen. John J. Pershing against the Mexican Revolutionary leader Pancho Villa. The Michigan soldiers were stationed near El Paso, Texas, from July 1916 to January 1917.

At dusk one evening a Michigan soldier on sentry duty called for the chaplain. He had been approached by a young Mexican whose wife was dying in childbirth. He had pleaded for a priest to perform last rites.

Dunigan listened to the story, quickly sought out the company doctor, and they followed the young husband to his adobe hut several miles into enemy territory. The two Americans ministered to the suffering woman all night and succeeded in saving her life and the child's as well. The grateful Mexican guided the soldiers back to their camp, but returned the next day. It seems he had told some of Villa's men of the chaplain's noble act, and they had sent him back to ask Dunigan "to please remove his hat as he rode along the border so they could see his bald head shine and their snipers would never make the mistake of shooting one so kind."

The experience and training that the men of the 32nd Infantry received while on duty on the Mexican border would help prepare them for a much greater test of their mettle - World War I.

President Woodrow Wilson had won re-election in 1916, thanks in part to his campaign slogan,"he kept us out of war." But Germany's unrestricted submarine warfare, which claimed the lives of Americans aboard vessels such as the *Lusitania*, inexorably drew the nation into the brutal conflict that had ravaged France and Belgium since 1914. On April 6, 1917, Congress declared war against Germany.

The allied war effort was then at a low point. American money, materiel and munitions soon helped restore allied morale, although it would be more than a year before appreciable numbers of U.S. combat troops fought alongside the French and British armies.

When war was declared the American army stood at a mere 200,000 men. By the war's end in November 1918, it had expanded more than twenty-fold. Some two million American troops served in France.

Following the declaration of war, volunteers swelled the 32nd Michigan National Guard to maximum strength. The Kalamazoo Armory on East Water Street was designated regimental headquarters, and Col. Westnedge assumed command of the unit. On July 15, 1917, all units of the Michigan National Guard were mustered into active federal service. A month later, movement of the regiments to the mobilization camp at Grayling began.

In Kalamazoo, Grand Rapids, Jackson, Flint and other Michigan cities where companies were located, crowds turned out to bid their soldier boys good-bye as they set out on their mission to win the "war to end all wars." "The farewells said, the trains steamed away amid waving handkerchiefs and flags, the ringing of bells and tooting of shop whistles, and here and there in the crowds could be seen an anxious mother, wife or sweetheart, with bowed head and moist eyes," wrote

Emil B. Gansser, a captain in the unit from Grand Rapids and author of the regimental history.

The guardsmen remained in intensive training at Camp Grayling until September 15th, when they were transferred to Camp McArthur, near Waco, Texas. There, the Michigan units were reorganized. The entire 32nd Michigan and elements of additional Michigan units became the 126th Infantry. Other Michigan companies composed the 125th Infantry. Those two units, supplemented with regiments from Wisconsin, formed the newly designated 32nd Division.

Not until February 1918, would the 32nd Division embark for France from New York on troop ships for a tense two-week long voyage, under threat of submarine attack. Then, for its first five months "Over There," the division suffered the humiliation of being broken up and assigned to various units to perform mundane supply duty. Of the 41 other divisions that went to war none had more esprit de corps than the 32nd. The Michigan and Wisconsin men wanted to see combat, to get the war over with.

During the Spring of 1918, a massive German offensive launched by Gen. Erich von Ludendorff had punched a bulge in the Allied lines that reached to within 50 miles of Paris by mid-July. French Gen. Ferdinand Foch, supreme commander of the western front, began a counter attack known as the Aisne-Marne Offensive on July 18. As part of that campaign, the men of the 32nd Division would finally earn their coveted combat experience - against battle-hardened German divisions - but at a terrific cost. At the end of their first day of battle, one out of every five of Dunigan's "boys" in the 126th Infantry would lie dead or wounded, a total of 460 casualties, and the others would never see the world in quite the same way again.

On July 30th, the 126th Infantry moved into the front line trenches along the Ourcq River. The next day, the Michigan men came under intense artillery fire while advancing to the northeast toward their objectives, the village of Cierges and the densely forested Jomblets Woods. The unit dug in for the night and at 3:30 the next morning went over the top in bloody bayonet charges against German machine gunners entrenched at the border of the Jomblets Woods. By night fall the 126th had forced its way 500 yards into the woods, a strategic coup that forced the Germans to

A 32nd Division doughboy named Cunningham sketched his recollections of the hand-to-hand fighting at the Battle of Meuse-Argonne.

retreat.

The intense hand-to-hand fighting continued over the succeeding four days as the 32nd Division served as an elite "shock division," to be hurled at the enemy "every time the Huns became obstinate and refused to budge from their stronghold." By August 6, the Aisne-Marne Offensive had resulted in an Allied victory, with the German bulge pushed back to a line that stretched from Soissons to Reims. The 32nd Division had suffered heavy casualties: 777 men killed and another 3,362 wounded.

Throughout the Michigan troops' five-day baptism of fire, Dunigan was to be found where the action was the fiercest, ministering to all who needed help regardless of their creed. At first he stuck a battered, shell-splintered crucifix into the ground at his position so those in need could locate him. But he could not resist clambering out over the barbed wire entanglement into the thick of battle. There, amid that shell-swept, gas-flooded hell he gave the last rites to dying boys, collected bundles of personal effects to be sent home to families in Michigan, carried bodies of the dead to where they would not be trampled under the feet of the advancing army and rigged over them crude crosses fashioned from shattered branches tied together with boot laces. Frequently, he served as a medic, tying tourniquets, bandaging bullet holes, adjusting gas masks on the wounded.

Westnedge urged his friend to take cover behind American lines, but he refused. When the shelling grew more intense, Dunigan sent his aide back to deliver the bundles of personal effects they had collected. The aide, Wallace Stanley from Grand Rapids, found his way back to the chaplain several times during the following two days, but each time Dunigan ordered him back out of harm's way as he continued his work on the battlefield. On the evening of the second day, Stanley lost track of Dunigan. The next day, while searching for him he encountered a wounded soldier returning from the front who told him how he had last seen the chaplain. Dunigan had been working steadily with the fallen soldiers during the advance, and as he was binding up the wounds of a young soldier he noticed the boy's gas mask was torn. Ripping off his own mask, he placed it on the soldier and said, "Buddy, you've had enough. You stand a chance, and you're not going to be gassed."

Dunigan donned the damaged gas mask just as a heavy wave of mustard gas swept over the field. He managed to crawl to higher ground where the gas was not as thick before collapsing. He lay there among the dead for 18 hours, when a burial detail discovered him and carried him to a field hospital.

Stanley traced him to the hospital where he found Dunigan breathing hard and painfully, his mouth packed with a greasy medication to help relieve the burning effects of the gas. "I'm fine and dandy," he gasped in a hoarse whisper, "fine and dandy."

Amazingly, the following night a motorcycle pulled up to the front line of the 126th, and out of the side car stepped Dunigan, shaky and pale, but ready for duty. He could not stay away from the action - "his boys might need him."

The men of the 32nd Division rested a few days after the Aisne-Marne Offensive then went into a brief training period before engaging in the Battle at Juvigny. Following that fierce struggle, the division remained in the thick of combat until the war's end. It compiled one of the most notable records of any American division, fighting on five fronts in three major offensives, during which it met and vanquished 23 German divisions. The 32nd Division adopted a red arrow as its insignia, signifying "that the division shot through every line the enemy put before it." Southwest Michigan's Red Arrow Highway commemorates the 32nd Division's valor. The unit was in action east of the Meuse River, when the armistice went into effect on November 11, 1918. During the six months it served under fire, with a mere 10 days in a rest area, the division suffered 14,000 casualties from all causes. Over 800 of its officers and men received decorations for valor from the American, French and Belgium governments.

Dunigan won a distinguished service cross for

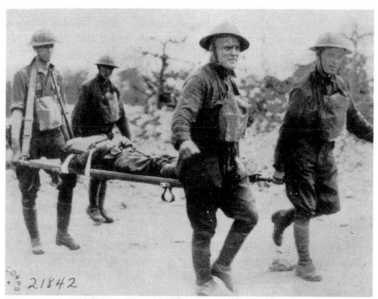

Stretcher bearers carry a wounded 126th Infantry soldier in 1918.

his "extraordinary heroism" during the Aisne-Marne Offensive. The French government awarded him three other medals for his valor throughout the war. Those and the purple hearts he was awarded for his head injury at Juvigny and a later shrapnel wound mark a military record rarely matched by a non-commandant.

Dunigan served with his regiment until the war's end. Tragically, a half hour before the armistice silenced the cannon's roar, a fellow 32nd Division chaplain, Father William F. Davitt, was killed. More crushing news followed the armistice. On November 29, Dunigan's close friend Westnedge died of complications inflicted by poison gas. Later, Kalamazoo residents renamed West Avenue in honor of their hometown hero and his brother Richard, who had died in the Spanish American War.

The 32nd Division was assigned occupation duty in Germany after the war, and Dunigan remained there until August 1919, when he returned to his priestly duties at St. Michael's in Flint. There, he took up the fight for whatever he knew to be right. The year 1920 found him lending his military hero's reputation to a campaign against a Michigan constitutional amendment which would have mandated all grade school children attend public schools. Voters defeated that "School Amendment" by a margin of nearly two to one.

In 1923, Dunigan was elevated to the rank of monsignor, and his parish duties in Flint and service state-wide took more and more of his time. But as the roaring twenties gave way to the Great Depression and thousands of unemployed World War I veterans marched to Washington in quest of federal assistance, Dunigan continued to savor a special relationship with his "boys" of the Red Arrow Division. He seemingly never forgot a face or the name of a veteran who had served with him. Once, a Detroit policeman was in the process of towing away an illegally parked car belonging to one of Dunigan's friends. Running up to the tow truck, the priest recognized the Irish cop as "one of his boys," and after he reminded him of a certain day in France when the two had shared the same dugout during an artillery barrage, the friend's automobile was promptly unhooked.

When saying mass at St. Michael's, Dunigan never failed to include a special prayer for "his boys" during that portion of the mass devoted to commemoration of the dead. He once told a friend, "I see the long ranks marching before me and please God, some day I will catch up with those lads of the 126th."

He was summoned to those ranks much too soon for the thousands in Flint and elsewhere who loved the gentle soldier priest. He was only 62-years-old when shortly before midnight on February 23, 1934, he suffered a cerebral hemorrhage. He died 55 minutes later.

As he lay in state, close to 15,000 mourners paid their last respects to Father Dunigan, filing reverently by his casket decorated with a floral representation of the flaming red arrow of the 32nd Division. Some 400 vehicles formed the funeral cortege that wound slowly through the streets of Flint, then on to Lapeer and finally into the little rural Kenochee Cemetery near Emmett.

There, he was laid to rest beside his parents and grandfather. The Springfield rifles of an American Legion honor squad barked their salute, and as the acrid smell of gunpowder drifted across the old cemetery, two buglers sounded the soul stirring notes of "taps."

Msgr. Duningan in later years.

Dr. Donald Hagerman, a long-time Kalamazoo dentist who grew up in Flint, remembered as a youth standing in awe on a street corner as Dunigan's long funeral procession rolled by. He also recalled how his World War I veteran father sometimes humorously ended their Depression era meals with a short grace and, "Thank you Lord, I'm Dunigan." Perhaps that is how the kindly chaplain would want to be remembered - with a joke and a smile.

The Influenza Pandemic of 1918

At first it was a joke - a funny sounding foreign word. Vaudeville comedians across the country quipped:

> *I had a little bird named Enza*
> *I opened the window and in—flu—enza!*

That was in the late summer of 1918. Then in September, influenza leaped across the ocean from the western front to the Atlantic seaboard, and newspaper headlines began marking the death toll. The laughter stopped.

Transmitted in March 1918 to Europe from China, where it had raged since 1910, the viral disease raced through the armies embroiled in World War I. The Germans called it *Blitzkatarrh*. The Allied forces named it the Spanish influenza because of a particularly virulent outbreak in Spain.

Its symptoms included fever and chills, sinus infections, pneumonia and encephalitis. Three distinct types emerged: (1) a very severe form with phenomenally rapid development and a fatal end within 36 - 48 hours; (2) a moderately severe onset with lung complications of a mild type, generally followed by easy recovery; (3) a mild beginning and quick improvement followed, however, after a few days, by a sudden rise in temperature and very serious results. The disease proved particularly fatal to pregnant women, children under two years old and, strangely, those between 20 and 40 years of age, who were slaughtered by the millions.

In America, it hit like a biological bombshell. By the end of 1918 at least 46 states were affected and ultimately one out of every four citizens fell ill. During mid-October, New York City reported 4,000 new cases and 250 deaths each day.

Particularly hard hit were army training camps. The death toll among U.S. armed forces surpassed 50,000, more than were killed in battle during the entire World War I.

The plague reached Michigan at the end of September. On October 1, 13 cases from southern Michigan had been reported to the Michigan Department of Health. The following day, 121 cases were reported, 90 of them from Jackson County. During the next three weeks, Jackson County continued to report more cases than any other Michigan county. Within that time, however, the disease struck practically every county in both peninsulas.

People began wearing face masks in public places. Authorities in Lansing advised against licking postage stamps and envelope flaps because of the dangers of infections. With no vaccine available, the U.S. Surgeon General issued a circular which, among other suggestions, advised people to breath through their nose instead of their mouth.

The number of cases and the death toll continued to soar. By October 18 nearly 2,000 new cases were being reported daily. On that date, Dr. R. M. Olin, commissioner of the Michigan Department of Health, issued an order closing churches, dance halls, poolrooms and all places of amusement and prohibiting public funerals or public gatherings of any kind.

The ban, in cojunction with mounting numbers of sick athletes and coaches, brought the cancellation of collegiate football schedules across the nation, including Western State Normal School (now WMU), Kalamazoo College, the University of Michigan and Notre Dame. As a result, the NCAA ruled the 1918 season not a factor in eligibility. Some players, such as Laurium native George Gipp, immortalized by Ronald Reagan in the classic film, "Knute Rockne - All American," were allowed to play five seasons on the

Battle Creek nursing students practiced donning face masks for work among influenza patients in 1918.

college gridiron.

Despite Michigan's ban, the toll continued to climb, reaching its peak on October 23 when more than 4,200 new cases were reported across the peninsulas. Finally the number of cases began to drop, and on November 7 the state lifted the ban on public gatherings.

In the meantime, Michigan's hospitals struggled to keep up with the patient load that clogged every room including hallways. The lack of available beds brought on by the epidemic motivated Detroit's Harper Hospital to change from an open to a closed hospital, thereby no longer admitting patients of doctors not on its staff. Butterworth Hospital in Grand Rapids overflowed with influenza cases, and even the student nurses found themselves working seven days a week, giving tepid sponge baths to patients and repeatedly changing perspiration-soaked bedding.

Borgess Hospital, which had dedicaated its new facility on Gull Road the year before, faced its greatest crisis since it opened as Kalamazoo's first hospital in 1889. The epidemic struck the nearby Nazareth community in early October. Thirty sisters fell ill as did scores of students at the two schools there.

The epidemic raced through the Student Army Training Corps candidates at Western State Normal School who had been crowded into a hastily-erected drafty barracks at the foot of Oakland Avenue. The Sisters of St. Joseph promptly placed the new hospital at the disposal of health officials who allocated an entire floor to the Western student sufferers. Every available sister in Kalamazoo reported for duty at the hospital.

With Bronson Hospital also overflowing with influenza victims, on October 17, the city health board opened an emergency hospital in the West South Street mansion of Althea Everard. During the following month, 79 patients were treated there.

Battle Creek faced a similar situation. In mid-October, the city leased the Richard Kingman dwelling on East Main Street to accommodate the overflow of patients from Nichols Hospital.

Particularly hard hit was nearby Camp Custer, which had opened as a training cantonment for drafted army troops the previous year. Poorly housed in crowded quarters, soldiers at Camp Custer began dropping like flies. The camp surgeon ordered each soldier's bunk draped with mosquito netting and personnel to sleep in alternate positions of head to toe so as not to breath on each other. Each trainee had his throat sprayed twice a day. Those primitive precautions brought little relief; 10,000 men at the camp contracted the disease - 663 died in October alone. By the year's end 841 soldiers had succumbed.

Many decades later, the children of Ernest L. Ferris, a Kalamazoo drayman, told stories of how their father was hired to cart corpses from the camp — at night so the public did not panic at the extent of the calamity.

As the year wore on the epidemic continued to rage across Michigan and the nation. December 31, 1918, saw nearly 2,000 new cases reported. Gradually, during the winter of 1919, the fury of the disease abated, although a less severe outbreak occurred the following winter. Michigan's final tally for the months of October, November and December 1918 documented 116,302 cases of influenza reported with 6,336 deaths. Another three to four thousand died from pneumonia as a secondary infection brought on by the influenza.

Rare was the American family unaffected by the viral holocaust. The worst pandemic of the century killed more than half a million Americans and some 20 million people worldwide.

Teenie Weenie's
In the North Country

Amidst the score of taverns, restaurants, hotels and gift shops that line the main street of Grand Marais, a pristine tourist mecca nestled beside one of Lake Superior's most beautiful harbors, stands a structure probably unique in architectural annals - a former residence and now the local chamber of commerce headquarters comprised of two big pickle barrels. And therein lies a story, a "Teenie Weenie" story.

The saga began in 1883 with the birth of William Donahey in Westchester, Ohio. A descendant of a prominent buckeye family that traces its American origins to an Irish immigrant who pioneered Ohio in 1799, Donahey developed into an imaginative and creative youth. At the age of eight he invented his own little army of flat headed screws. He dabbed red paint on one and called it the general. Another screw with an uneven head that continually toppled over he dubbed the dunce. Fascinated with the toilers at a local Chinese laundry, he fashioned a queue out of a bit of string, and that screw became the Chinaman.

But Donahey's childish imagination sometimes landed him in trouble with his stern Methodist parents. Once, while the family entertained a distinguished guest for dinner, Donahey grew bored with the conversation and retreated to his own world of little people. Imagining one tiny creature gamboling across the table settings and tumbling head first into the gravy boat, he laughed out loud. In an era when children were to be "seen but not heard," that infraction brought chastisement from his mother who warned he "would never amount to anything for harboring such trifling thoughts." She was wrong.

As a teenager Donahey showed artistic talent and his parents decided he should emulate his older brother Hal's career as a commercial artist. Following study at the Cleveland School of Art, where, as he later declared, "I didn't learn a damn thing - had to teach myself all over again," he got a job with an advertising firm. By 1903 he had joined his brother as an artist on the staff of the Cleveland *Plain Dealer.* There he honed his artistic skills by drawing a color page for the Sunday issue and through daily assignments.

In 1905, Donahey wed Mary Dickerson, a feature writer at the *Plain Dealer* and ultimately an author of numerous children's books. Mary's success may have inspired Donahey to try his hand at the genre of juvenile literature. In reaction to the contemporary comic strips which frequently depicted characters getting kicked down stairs, beaten up and suffering as the butt of other violent jokes, he saw the need for a more humane approach. But it took a year of lobbying before the *Plain Dealer's* managing editor could be persuaded to try something new. Finally, in 1910, he relented, allotting Donahey a page a week.

Donahey filled the page with his modernized version of Mother Goose rhymes. His illustrations and text scored an immediate hit with the public, and the series ran for five years. By 1914 the popular Mother Goose page had come to the attention of legendary Chicago *Tribune* editor Joseph Medill Patterson who invited Donahey to submit a weekly series. The artist transformed his childhood screw characters into a two-inch high race he called the Teenie Weenies. The little folks, including a general, a clumsy dunce, a peg-legged old veteran, a lady of fashion, a poet, a policeman, a Chinaman and about 20 other named characters, dwelt in a shoe house under a rose bush. They lived on the periphery of human society, adapting cast-off items to their needs, interacting with friendly mice, squirrels and birds, hunting frogs, fishing, conducting warfare against a neighboring tribe of diminutive savages and enjoying lives of mischief and adventure unbeknownst to their giant counterparts.

Patterson was so enchanted with the concept that he defied a newspaper maxim and ordered advertisements moved to another section of the paper to accommodate the Teenie Weenies. The overwhelming

Boiling an egg in Teenie Weenie Land required hard work and ingenuity.

public response to the trial run moved the editor to feature the series in four colors in the Sunday magazine section. In large part due to the Teenie Weenie's popularity, the *Tribune's* Sunday circulation doubled by 1921.

The Donaheys moved to Chicago, where William enjoyed the luxury of working at home exclusively on the Teenie Weenies. Beginning in 1916, Donahey began publishing Teenie Weenie stories in illustrated book format. Eleven titles appeared over the next three decades, including school textbooks recounting Teenie Weenie exploits. The St. Louis *Republican* and other papers began running Donahey's series, and following syndication of the Teenie Weenies in 1923, some 30 newspapers across the United States and Canada furthered the wee people's popularity.

Sensing the commercial appeal of the Teenie Weenies, the Reid-Murdock Company, a mammoth packaged food conglomerate that marketed Monarch brand products, commissioned Donahey to design packages, labels and mass circulation magazine advertisements for a new Teenie Weenie line of canned goods, breakfast cereal, peanut butter, and pickles packed in miniature wooden barrels.

Newspaper work, book royalties and, especially, advertising commissions made the childless Donaheys wealthy. The couple bought a big house in a fashionable Chicago neighborhood. In 1925, S.P. Stevens, a vice president of Reid-Murdock who had long vacationed at Grand Marais, introduced the Donaheys to that idyllic part of the Upper Peninsula. The cartoonist purchased a tract on the shore of nearby Grand Sable Lake.

Stevens decided to present the couple with a gift he could incidently parley into advertising copy: a cottage in the form of a giant version of the barrels Teenie-Weenie pickles came in. A Chicago cooperage firm

**The Donaheys posed before their Teenie Weenie barrel-house
on the shore of Grand Sable Lake.**

designed the structure from 16-foot and eight-foot high barrels. The big barrel featured a living room with a spiral stairway leading to the upstairs bedroom. A passageway connected a fully equipped kitchen in the smaller barrel. The firm shipped the big staves by rail to Seney and trucked them to the site where a foundation had been laid.

Stevens drove the Donaheys north, in late spring 1926, to unveil his surprise. Arriving in Grand Marais, he suggested a hike along the shore of Grand Sable Lake. It was near dusk when they spotted the strange structure. As they approached, a troupe of Grand Marais children dressed like Teenie Weenies marched up. After reciting a poem welcoming the Donaheys, they presented the key to the barrel house.

The unique cottage became the talk of the north country. The day the Donahey's moved in, more than 200 uninvited guests arrived to tour it. Publicity in the *Saturday Evening Post* and other periodicals brought Stevens the promotion he sought but also a never ending stream of "fudgies." Sunday soon became particularly hectic for the couple who valued their privacy. To avoid visitors, they developed a routine of locking the cottage and hiding in the woods.

The Donaheys managed to cope with unwanted gawkers for ten summers before, in exasperation, they gave the barrel house to a local merchant. He knocked it down and moved it to Grand Marais. The Donaheys constructed a simple log cabin on the site, where they enjoyed blissfully quiet vacations until Mary's death in 1958. William continued his Teenie-Weenie newspaper features until he died in 1969.

And in remote Grand Marais, the big barrel house still stands as a reminder of the once popular tiny cartoon people's connection with the north country.

Everyman's House

Perhaps not one in a thousand of the motorists who zoom up Kalamazoo's Westnedge Avenue Hill each day cast even a glance at the unobtrusive little colonial house they pass. But in 1924, when Star touring cars, Whippets, Overlands and locally-produced Roamers vied with the streetcars that ran up the center of the street, "Everyman's House" drew national attention.

The building gained fame not through connection with some well-known personality or as the scene of a grisly murder, but simply because of its unassuming architecture. And many years later, the chronicle of Everyman's House continues to offer a more sophisticated citizenry important lessons about family values and what is really important in life.

The saga of the storied structure began when Caroline Bartlett Crane, prominent social activist and wife of Kalamazoo's pioneer radiologist, Dr. Augustus W. Crane, received an invitation from Secretary of Commerce Herbert Hoover to participate in a national "Better Homes in America" contest. The competition sought innovative architectural ideas that might lead to better housing for average American families. The entries were to be built for about $5,000.

Crane, then 65 and busy raising two adopted children, had shelved many activities that earlier earned her honors as an advocate for better meat inspection, clean streets and as "municipal housekeeper to the nation." But this cause struck a chord. The plight of harried homemakers, laboring tirelessly under adverse conditions with naught in the way of time-saving devices and little assistance from family members, had long troubled her. The old warrior answered the tocsin with passion.

Crane called a meeting of potential participants on March 3, 1924, and met with ebullient enthusiasm.

Based partly on subcommittee recommendations, she sketched out the designs for the structure. Local architect Gilbert Worden translated her ideas into site plans and elevations. The Kalamazoo Realtors' Association provided a lot in what was then suburban Kalamazoo, across from Crane Park (named not after Caroline but an unrelated namesake, Edgar Crane). Local lumber yards and hardware stores supplied materials. A general contractor, plumbers, electricians, furnace installers and other public-minded Kalamazoo businessmen "cheerfully agreed to furnish anything and everything wanted, charge it up at the regular retail price, and wait for their pay until the house should be used in demonstrations and then sold." An interior decorator and a landscape architect pledged to follow the recommendations of Crane's committees.

Crane rushed the project along to meet the contest deadline. The ground-breaking ceremony came on March 13th. Eleven days later, a mason laid the cornerstone. On May 12th, the first day of the national "Better Homes" week, a carpenter drove the last nail, and the contractor handed over the keys. Then came a dedicatory lighting of the hearth. The team had accomplished the entire endeavor, including interior decorating and landscaping, in less than two months.

Everyman's House, designed for a family of five children "in which the father has a hard time making both ends meet and the mother does all the work in the house," was diminutive by modern standards. A story and a half on a full basement, it measured just 22-feet by 29-feet. But as one realtor remarked, "It's the biggest little house I ever saw!"

Crane had achieved her goals by designing a compact floor plan that eliminated hallways. Instead, room entrances and stairs to the second floor bedrooms flowed from a vestibule. She laid out the kitchen, "the hub of the household," to increase efficiency and to eliminate "extra steps." The living room, complete with fireplace and a seven-foot window seat, doubled as the dining room. The traditional dining room had been replaced by a downstairs bedroom, which Crane termed the "mother's suite," located adjacent the kitchen. When used as a nursery, it saved a mother from constantly climbing to the upstairs bedrooms. Dwellings of this era normally boasted but one bath-

The dust jacket of Crane's 1925 book.

room, situated on the second floor. But Crane placed it downstairs, next to the mother's suite for child-rearing convenience.

The first home genuinely planned for the needs of the housewife, Everyman's House was a "space-saving, step-saving, time-saving, money-saving small house built around the mother and baby." A passway counter saved the cook from lugging each dish from the kitchen to the dining table. A convenient stool allowed a women to deal with the meal's "dreary, dreadful, stupid anti-climax - the dishes" while sitting. And a picture window over the sink, which no architect had previously conceived, allowed working women to view the outside world.

Despite her own career as a social activist, Crane saw no reason to apologize for women who chose to contribute to the family's welfare as house-wives. Rather, she applauded their devotions. She offered Everyman's House as "a plant for the manufac-ture of good citizens," designed to make household tasks easier.

In the weeks following its dedication, a corps of 85 hostesses interpreted the novel home to some 20,000 people who trooped through. Visitors marveled at avante garde features, including a built-in, recessed bathtub that eliminated the arduous task of cleaning behind the old type claw-foot tub, a clothes chute to the basement laundry room, a basement shower stall, auto-matic water heater, water softener and luxerious soap-stone laundry tubs. Numerous wall plugs permitted better lighting via reading lamps than the traditional shadowy chandeliers. The big brick fireplace blazed as the heart of the living/dining room.

But expensive amenities and the use of extra-quality materials such as solid oak flooring, brass and nickel plated hardware and superior roofing and siding pushed the project considerably over budget. The bottom line for the little home reached $7,249.51. The lot ran another $1,000. While seemingly reasonable by modern standards, in 1924 a new Model T Ford sold for $300 or less. Based on a contemporary compact new car-to-home ratio, Everyman's House would cost $330,000.

Despite the construction overrun, which Crane suggested might be remedied by eliminating some of the home's ultra-modern options, she received a joyful announcement from Hoover on June 25, 1924. Out of 1,500 entries from across the nation, Everyman's House had placed first. President Calvin Coolidge sent Crane a congratulatory letter, noting that: "The home has been and ever must be a source of profound influence and inspiration in the lives of all citizens. It plays a chief role in the development of the children of our nation for stability and uprightness."

Articles in nationally circulated magazines praised Kalamazoo's "revolutionary house." In 1925, Crane published her account of the project as a 226 page book, *Everyman's House*. In it she wrote: "The greatest need of almost every city is to increase the precious quota of its steady, responsible, home-owning citizens."

Crane's work, no doubt, influenced many working class Kalamazooans to pursue dreams of home ownership. In the late 1930s, sociologist Edward Thorndike evaluated home ownership and other criteria to rank Kalamazoo among the top ten American cities for general quality of life. The 1950 federal census verified that more than two-thirds of the city's homes were owned by the people living in them.

Ironically, Caroline Bartlett Crane, who had campaigned so valiantly to prevent women needless trips up and down stairs, suffered a heart attack and toppled down the stairs of her home to her death in 1935.

The Football Game
that Should Never
Have Been Played

It was 1934, the depth of the Depression. Few Michigan residents had much to cheer about - certainly not the University of Michigan football fans who would watch their team blunder though its worst season of the century. Despite the leadership of their tough captain, Gerald R. Ford, the Wolverine eleven won but one game that fall - and that was a game that should never have been played.

Beginning in 1901, Coach Fielding "Hurry Up" Yost had launched Michigan's golden era of the gridiron. His "point a minute" teams set records yet to be broken. Born in West Virginia, the son of a Confederate veteran, Yost fell in love with the game of football. Unfortunately, he carried some southern baggage to his northern coaching career: a deep-seated racial prejudice.

While George H. Jewett, an Ann Arbor High School star, had broken the color barrier to letter on the Wolverine team in 1890, during Yost's 25 years as head football coach his teams included not one black athlete. Yost stepped down as football coach after the 1926 season but continued as athletic director. Still, the racial situation remained unchanged until the appointment as head football coach of former Michigan All-American Harry Kipke in 1929. Kipke, who had played with black team mates at Lansing High School, had a different philosophy.

That is when Willis Ward entered the picture. One of the greatest athletes to come out of Detroit's Northwestern High School, Ward won the city high jump title as a freshman. He went on to set state records in the low and high hurdles, and as a junior he bested the world interscholastic high jump mark.

Voted an all-city end for two years, he earned unanimous selection to the all-state football team in his senior year. An A student, Ward graduated near the top of his class.

Realizing he had no chance to play football for Michigan, Ward debated going to Dartmouth or Northwestern University. But when Wayne County Circuit Court Judge Guy Miller, a Michigan alumnus, learned of the situation, he conferred with Michigan Regents James Murfin and Fred Matthai, president of the University of Michigan Club in Detroit. They decided to buck the system.

After Ward agreed to try to end the team segregation, they approached Kipke, who responded, "You're darn right I'll take that kid." But Kipke faced an uphill battle against Yost and some coaches and alumni who could not understand why Michigan needed a black football player - the team had won many a game without one. As Ward later learned, "on several occasions Kipke took his coat off and was prepared to fight with those who bitterly opposed having a Negro play for Michigan."

The feisty Kipke, with the backing of Miller, Murfin and Matthai, prevailed. Ward enrolled as one of about 30 black students on campus. When he showed up at the field house to be assigned a locker, Judge Miller's son, captain of the swim team, met him. "I'm Bob Miller," he said, "my father told me you were coming, and if you have any problems, let me know." Kipke also encouraged other key athletes to smooth Ward's way.

Kipke found a much needed part-time job for Ward washing dishes at the Parrot Cafe. But when the manager ordered him to only use the back door and Ward told his coach, Kipke got him a better job washing dishes at the Michigan Union.

Ward soon proved that Kipke's trust had not been misplaced. Starting as a right end in 1932 and

1933, he was named to the Big Ten and National Championship teams both years. The following season he made the second team All-American roster. And in track, he consistently set records in the high hurdles, dash and high jump. In 1935, he beat Ohio State's Jesse Owens in the 65 yard high hurdles and tied a world record by outracing Owens in the 60 yard dash.

Sometime in 1933, as Ward wowed track and football crowds, Yost scheduled a match in Ann Arbor for the 1934 fall season with Georgia Tech, then coached by his good friend William A. Alexander. By December 1933 correspondence between Yost and other southern coaches centered around "what he was going to do about the detail." The detail being that

Willis Ward as he appeared in a 1934 U of M game program.

Georgia Tech and most other southern collegiate teams had never played against black opponents and had no intention of doing so in the future.

It was era when many northern schools, including Ohio State and NYU, routinely bowed to that prejudice by benching their black players. Others, such as Harvard and Dartmouth, refused to be a part of the racism. What would the University of Michigan do?

Negotiations continued through the winter of 1934. Georgia Tech took the stance that if Ward was to play they would cancel the game. Michigan was reminded that as a "well bred host" out of courtesy it should take the feelings of Georgia Tech into consideration. In January, Michigan's Board in Control of Athletics discussed at length the racial implications of the match but reached no conclusion. In May, with no decision yet made, Georgia Tech remained adamant in its position.

Ward had returned home to Detroit for the summer vacation when he learned the outcome - he would not get to play against Georgia Tech. Sensitive and proud, he wrote Coach Kipke that he was quitting the football team. Kipke rushed to Detroit to explain that Georgia Tech absolutely would not play against a black. Then he reminded Ward of the battles he and others had fought to get him on the team and said that he would never do so for another black if Ward quit. Crestfallen, Ward agreed to stay on the team.

Roy Wilkins, assistant secretary of the NAACP, and some Michigan alumni, campaigned on Ward's behalf to no avail. As the October 20th game date drew near, five Jewish sophomores organized "The United Front Committee on Ward." University of Michigan students staged a massive rally on Friday. That night hundreds of students marched eight miles to demonstrate outside the Ypsilanti hotel where the visiting Yellowjackets were lodged.

Yost had heard rumors of a planned student sit-down in the middle of the football field during the game. He hired a Pinkerton detective to identify the ring leaders and sent a number of students to infiltrate the rally and disrupt the sit-down plans. Still, the strength of the student movement continued to worry him.

Legendary Georgia Tech coach "Bobby" Dodd, then an assistant to Alexander, remembered in his 1987 autobiography how Yost and Alexander debated the dilemma over a bottle of whiskey, well into the night. Alexander kept saying, "We cannot play the game against a black man. We could not go back to Atlanta."

Finally, the coaches negotiated a compromise. Ward would not play but neither would Georgia's star right end, E. H. "Hoot" Gibson. Joint announcements Saturday morning that Ward and Gibson had "volunteered" to sit out the game defused the explosive situation.

That afternoon, a one-third capacity crowd watched what Dodd recalled "as poorly played a game between two major college teams as I've ever seen." Michigan won 9 to 2. Ward had been refused permission to watch the game from the bench or press box. He sat out the event in the fraternity house.

Following the game, the *Michigan Daily* editorialized: "Michigan's principles are incompatable with the South's position on racial differences. Let Michigan of the future play with those who are of her own eminently worthwhile type." The Georgia Tech game became a *cause celebre* on campus. University President Alexander Ruthven confided to a friend, "My life is being made miserable by arguments with the colored brethren... I wish now that I had taken the Ward matter into my own hands."

As a result, Michigan did not play another southern football team for 19 years. And it would be seven years before another black athlete, Julius Franks, would play for the Michigan eleven.

As for Willis Ward, in a 1970 interview he said, "That Georgia Tech game knocked me right square in the gut. It was wrong. It will always be wrong, and it killed my desire to excel."

Nevertheless, Ward would excel in later life. Following graduation, he worked for the Ford Motor Company. Attending night school, he earned a law degree in 1939. He became assistant prosecutor for Wayne County, sat on the first governing board of Northern Michigan University and for six years served as chairman of the Michigan Public Service Commission. In 1973, Governor William Milliken appointed him as the first black judge of probate for Wayne County. When Ward died in 1984, his old team-mate, former President Ford, said, "I have lost one of my dearest friends... He was truly a great American in every way. He contributed so much to a better society in America."

One other thing about the black hero who suffered the humiliation of racism in 1934 should be mentioned. Ward, who had an excellent chance of taking gold medals in the high jump, hurdles and decathlon, refused to participate in the 1936 Berlin Olympics because of Hitler's anti-semitism. A quarter century later, Ward said: "It was just as bad as if they'd done it to the blacks, to me, what they did to the Jews. I've never regretted not having competed in the Olympics."

SOURCES

Voyage to the Land of the Stinkers

Butterfield, Consul W. *History of the Discovery of the Northwest by John Nicolet...* Cincinnati, 1881.

Dever, Harry. "The Nicolet Myth," *Michigan History.* Vol. 50. No. 4. (December 1966). p. 318.

Dunbar, Willis & May, George. *Michigan A History of the Wolverine State.* Grand Rapids, [1980].

Garneau, F.H. & Ferland, J.B. "Jean Nicolet," *Wisconsin Historical Collections.* Vol. X (1883-1885). p. 41.

Hodge, Frederick Webb. *Handbook of American Indians...* 2 Vols. .Washington, 1912..

John Nicolet: Exercises At the Unveiling of the Tablet... Lansing, 1915.

Moore, Charles. *The Northwest Under Three Flags.* New York, 1900.

Neville, Ella, Martin, Sarah & Martin, Deborah. *Historic Green Bay.* Green Bay, 1893.

Pittman, Philip M. *The Les Cheneaux Chronicles.* (Charlevoix, 1984).

Story, Norah. *The Oxford Companion to Canadian History & Literature.* Toronto, 1967.

Sulte, Benjamin. "Notes on Jean Nicolet," *Wisconsin Historical Collections.* Vol. VII . (1879). p. 188.

Winsor, Justin. *Cartier to Frontenac...* Boston, 1894.

Wood Edwin O. *Historic Mackinac...* 2 Vols. New York, 1918.

Lacrosse: Michigan's First Team Sport

Charlevoix, P. Francois-Xavier. *Journal of A Voyage to North America.* 2 Vols. London, 1761.

Catlin, George. *North American Indians...* 2 Vols. Philadelphia, 1913.

Culin, Stewart, "Games of the North American Indians" *Bureau of American Ethnology.* 24th Annual Report. Washington, 1907.

Evans, G.H. & Anderson, Robert E. *Lacrosse Fundamentals.* South Brunswick, N.J. [1966].

Grant, Peter, "The Sauteux Indians," in Masson, L.R. *Bourgeois de la Compagnie du Nord-Quest...* 2 Vols. Quebec, 1889-90.

Hodge, Frederick Webb. *Handbook of American Indians...* 2 Vols. Washington, 1912.

Jones, William, "Notes on the Fox Indians," *Iowa Journal of History & Politics.* Vol. 10. No. 1 [Jan. 1912].   p. 70.

Kinietz, W. Vernon. *Chippewa Village.* Bloomfield Hills, [1947].

_____. *The Indians of the Western Great Lakes. 1615-1760.* Ann Arbor, 1940.

Sabrevois, Monsieur de. "Memoir On the Savages of Canada...," *Wisconsin Historical Collections.* Vol. XVI [1902]. p. 363.

Schoolcraft, Henry Rowe. *Historical...Information Respecting the ... Indian Tribes...* 6 Vols. Philadelphia, 1851-57.

Thwaites, Reuben G. "The Wisconsin Winnebagoes," *Wisconsin Historical Collections.* Vol. XII [1892]. p. 399.

Trowbridge, C.C. *Meearmeear Traditions.* Ann Arbor, 1938.

Madam Laframboise: Queen of the Fur Trade

Baird, Elizabeth Therese. "Reminiscences of Early Days On Mackinac Island,"*Wisconsin Historical Collections.*Vol. XIV (1898). p.17

Goss, Dwight. "The Indians of the Grand River Valley,"*Michigan Pioneer Collections.* Vol. XVII (1905). p. 172.

Havighurst, Walter. *Three Flags At The Straits.* Englewood Cliffs, N.J., [1966].

McDowell, John E. "Madam LaFramboise," *Michigan History.* Vol. LVI. No. 4. (Winter, 1972). p. 271.

Rezek, Antoine Ivan. *History of the Diocese of Sault Ste. Marie & Marquette.* 2 Vols. Houghton, 1907.

Widder, Keith R. "Magdelaine Laframboise, Fur Trader & Educator," in Troester, Rosalie Riegle, ed. *Historic Women of Michigan A Sesquicentennial Celebration.* Lansing, [1987].

Wood, Edwin O. *Historic Mackinac...* 2 Vols. New York, 1918

Charles Hoffman's Ride Across the Peninsula

Hoffman, Charles F. *A Winter in the Far West.* 2 Vols. London, 1835.

Holt, Lucius H. "Hoffman, Charles Fenno," *Dictionary of American Biography.* Vol. IX. New York, 1932.

Kunitz, Stanley J. & Haycraft, Howard, eds. *American Authors 1600-1900...* New York, 1938.

Snakes Alive: The Birth of Allegan

Armstrong, Joe & Pahl, John. *River & Lake: A Sesquicentennial History of Allegan County, Michigan.* [Allegan, 1985].

Blois, John T. *Gazetteer of Michigan...* Detroit, 1838.

Ditmars, Raymond L. *A Field Book of North American Snakes.* New York, 1949.

[Johnson, Crisfield]. *History of Allegan & Barry Counties.* Philadelphia, 1880.

Michigan Biographies. 2 Vols. Lansing, 1924.

Morgan, G.A. "The Township of Allegan - Its Topography, Products, Early Settlement, & History," *Michigan Pioneer Collections.* Vol. 3 (1881). p. 276.

Murray, Janette & Frederick. T*he Story of Cedar Rapids.* New York, 1950.

Schoolcraft, Henry Rowe. *Personal Memoirs of A Residence of Thirty Years...* Philadelphia, 1851.

Thomas, Henry. *Twentieth Century History of Allegan County.* Chicago, 1907.

Williams, Benjamin O. "Address at the Oakland County Reunion," *Michigan Pioneer Collections*. Vol. 14 (1889). p. 510.

Potatoes, Pork & Pone: Pioneer Cookery

Bingham, Stephen D. "Memoir of Anson De Peuy Van Buren," *Michigan Pioneer Collections*. Vol. 22 (1893). p. 217.

Buley, R. Carlyle. *The Old Northwest. Pioneer Period 1815-1840*. 2 Vols. Bloomington, Ind., 1950.

Chase, Alvin W. *Dr. Chase's Recipes...* Ann Arbor, 1864.

Kirkland, Caroline. *A New Home Who'll Follow!* New York, 1839.

Ellet, Elizabeth. *Pioneer Women of the West*. New York, 1852.

Gray, Mrs. Martha. "Reminiscences of Grand Traverse Region," *Michigan Pioneer Collections*. Vol. 38 (1912). p. 285.

Hayes, Mrs. A.M. "Reminiscences of Pioneer Days in Hastings," *Michigan Pioneer Collections*. Vol. 26 (1896).   p. 235.

Van Buren, Anson D.P. "Titus Bronson, The Founder of   Kalamazoo," *Michigan Pioneer Collections*. Vol. 5 (1882). p. 363.

_____. "What the Pioneers Ate & How They Fared...," *Michigan Pioneer Collections*. Vol. 5 (1882). p. 293.

Charles Lanman, Michigan's First Native-Born Author of Distinction

Bulkley, John M. *History of Monroe County, Michigan...* 2 Vols. Chicago, 1913.

Lanman, Charles. *Adventures in the Wilds of the United   States & British American Provinces*. 2 Vols. Phildelphia, 1856.

_____. *Dictionary of the United States Congress...* Philadelphia, 1859.

_____. *Essays For Summer Hours*. 2nd ed. Boston , 1842.

_____. *Farthest North...* New York, 1885.

_____. *Haphazard Personalities: Chiefly of Noted Americans*. Boston & New York, 1886.

_____. *Haw-Ho-Noo; or Records of a Tourist.*   Philadelphia, 1850.

_____. *The Life of William Woodbridge*. Washington, 1867.

_____. *The Red Book of Michigan; A Civil, Military & Biographical History*. Detroit, 1871.

_____. *A Summer in the Wilderness*. New York, 1847.

Orchard, Harry Frederick. *Charles Lanman Landscapes & Nature Studies*. Catalog of Morris Museum of Arts & Sciences Exhibit. Morristown, New Jersey, 1983,

Pageant of Historic Monroe, June 23-24. N.P., 1926.

Wilson, James G. & Fiske, John. *Appleton's Cyclopedia of American Biography*. 6 Vols. New York, 1888.

The Saga of the Ontonagon Boulder

Bald, F. Clever. *Michigan In Four Centuries.* New York, [1954].

Foster, J.W. & Whitney, J.D. *Report on the Geology & Topography of a Portion of the Lake Superior Land District... Part 1. Copper Lands.* Washington, 1850.

Hybels, Robert James. "The Lake Superior Copper Fever, 1841-47," *Michigan History Magazine.* Vol. 34. No. 2. (June 1950). p. 97.

Jamison, James K. *The Ontonagon Country.* Ontonagon, [1948].

Krause, David J. *The Making of A Mining District: Keweenaw Native Copper 1500-1870.* Detroit, [1992].

Murdock, Angus. *Boom Copper.* New York, 1943.

Schoolcraft, Henry Rowe. *Narrative Journal of Travels From Detroit Northwest...* Albany, 1821.

Caroline Quarreles' Flight to Freedom

Barnes, Charles E. "Battle Creek As Station on the Underground Railway," *Michigan Pioneer Collections.* Vol. 38 [1912]. p. 279.

Bergman, Peter M. *The Chronological History of the Negro in America.* New York, [1969].

[Durant, Samuel]. *History of Kalamazoo County...* Philadelphia, 1880.

Holmes, Fred L. *Badger Saints & Sinners.* Milwaukee, [1939].

Olin, C.C. *Complete Record of the John Olin Family.* Indianapolis, 1893.

When Doomsday Came & Went

Devens, R.M. *The Great Events of the Past Century.* Tecumseh, MI., 1879.

Carson, Gerald. *Cornflake Crusade.* New York, [1957].

Dick, Everett N. "Miller, William," *Dictionary of American Biography.* Vol. XII. New York, 1933. p. 641.

[Durant, Samuel]. *History of Kalamazoo County.* Philadelphia, 1880.

Larrabee, Harold R. "The Trumpeter of Doomsday," *American Heritage.* Vol. XV. No. 3 (April 1964). p. 35.

Loughborough, J.N. *The Great Second Advent Movement: Its Rise & Progress.* Nashville, Tenn., [1905].

Newton, Chris. "Church Awaits God's Arrival in Dallas Suburb." *Kalamazoo Gazette.* 5 March 1998.

Olsen, M. Ellsworth. *A History of the Origin & Progress of Seventh-Day Adventists.* Takoma Park, Washington, [1925].

Pilcher, Elijah H. *Protestantism in Michigan...* Detroit, [1878].

Van Buren, A.D.P. "Caleb Eldred - Sketch of His Life & Services," *Michigan Pioneer Collections.* Vol. 5 (1882). p. 387.

White, James. *Sketches of the Christian Life & Public Labors of William Miller.* Battle Creek, 1875.

Testy Trollope's Travels

Dunbar, Willis F. *All Aboard! A History of Railroads in Michigan.* Grand Rapids, [1969].

Faust, Patrica L. ed. *Historical Times Illustrated Encyclopedia of the Civil War.* New York, [1986].

Garnett, Richard. "Anthony Trollope" in *Dictionary of National Biography.* New York, 1909. Vol. 19, p. 1165.

Hubach, Robert R. *Early Midwestern Travel Narratives: An Annotated Bibliography 1634-1850.* Detroit, 1961.

James, Henry. "Anthony Trollope," *Century Magazine.* New Series Vol. IV (1883). p. 385.

Kunitz, Stanley J. & Haycroft, Howard, eds. *British Authors of the Nineteenth Century.* New York, 1936.

Lillie, Leo C. *Historic Grand Haven & Ottawa County.* Grand Haven, 1931.

Nevins, Allan, ed. *American Social History As Recorded by British Travellers.* New York, (1923).

Seibold, David H. *Coast Guard City, U.S.A. A History of the Port of Grand Haven.* [Ann Arbor, 1990].

Trollope, Anthony. *North America.* 3 Vols. Leipzig, 1862.

Trollope, [Frances]. *Domestic Manners of the Americans.* London, 1832.

Tuckerman, Henry F. *America & Her Commentators...* New York, 1864.

The White Widow Among the Chippewa

Clifton, James, Cornell, George,and McClurken, James. *People of the Three Fires. The Ottawa, Potawatomi & Ojibway of Michigan.* [Grand Rapids, 1986].

McClurken, James M. *A Visual Culture History of the Little Traverse Bay Bands of Odawa.* East Lansing, [1991].

Reuter, Dorothy. *Methodist Indian Ministries in Michigan, 1830-1990.* Grand Rapids, [1983].

[Sagatoo, Mary]. *Wah Sash Kah Moqua; or Thirty-Three Years Among the Indians.* Boston, 1897.

A Michigan Civil War Florence Nightingale

Faust, Patricia L. *Historical Times Illustrated Encyclopedia of the Civil War.* New York, [1986].

Goodsell, Charles True & Dunbar, Willis F. *Centennial History of Kalamazoo College.* Kalamazoo, 1933.

McTeer, Frances Davis. "In Bonnet & Shawl" in *Michigan Women in the Civil War.* N.P. [1963].

Record of Eighth Michigan Infantry, Civil War. [Kalamazoo, 1903].

Robertson, John. *Michigan In the War.* Lansing, 1882.

Wheelock, Julia. *The Boys in White...* New York, 1876.

The Shooting of Sheriff Orcutt

Atlas of Kalamazoo Co. Michigan. New York, 1873.

Confidential $500.00 Reward For the Arrest & Delivery of Stephen Boyle... N.P., [1867].

[Durant, Samuel]. *History of Kalamazoo County, Michigan.* Philadelphia, 1880.

Portrait & Biographical Record of Kalamazoo, Allegan & Van Buren Counties, Michigan. Chicago, 1892.

Thomas, James M. *Kalamazoo County Directory...* Kalamazoo, 1869.

"Curfew Must Not Ring Tonight"

Burke, W.J. & Howe, Will D. *American Authors & Books 1640 to the Present.* New York, [1962].

Hillsdale Area Centennial 1869-1969 N.P., [1969].

Hopkins, A.A. *Waifs & Their Authors.* Boston, [1879].

James, George Wharton. *Rose Hartwick Thorpe & the Story of "Curfew Must Not Ring To-Night."* Pasadena, Cal., [1916].

Of Goats, Gillens & Green Gold

Ayer, N.W., ed. *America Newspaper Annual & Directory.* Philadelphia, 1910.

Beck, E.C. *Lore of the Lumber Camps.* Ann Arbor, 1948.

Collins, James. *Life in a Lumber Camp.* Alpena, 1914.

First Report of the Directors of the State Forestry Commission of Michigan. Lansing, 1888.

Fuller, George N., ed. *Historic Michigan, Land of the Great Lakes.* Vol. 3: *Local Histories of Several Michigan Counties.* Dayton, Ohio, N.D.

Haltiner, Robert. *The Town That Wouldn't Die.* N.P., N.D.

Holbrook, Stewart H. *Holy Old Mackinaw.* New York, 1938.

Powers, Perry F. *A History of Northern Michigan.* 3 Vols. Chicago, 1912.

Sorden, L.G. *Lumberjack Lingo.* Spring Green, Wisconsin, [1969].

When a "Sucker" Pulled the Plug of Crystal Lake

Case, Leonard. *Benzie County: A Bicentennial Reader.* [Cadillac, 1976].

Case, W.L. *The Tragedy of Crystal Lake...* Beulah, 1976.

Catton, Bruce. *Waiting for the Morning Train: An American Boyhood.* New York, 1972.

Powers, Perry F. *A History of Northern Michigan.* 3 Vols. Chicago, 1912.

The Day Michigan Burned Its Thumb

Du Mond, Neva. *Thumb Diggings.* Lexington, [1962].

Holbrook, Stewart H. *Burning an Empire.* New York, 1943.

Lincoln, James H. & Donahue, James L. *Fiery Trail.* Ann Arbor, [1984].

Park, Roderick. *The Thumb Fire of 1881.* [Sault Ste. Marie, 1955].

Raymond, Oliver. *Shingle Shavers & Berry Pickers.* N.P., [1976].

Schultz, Gerard. *The New History of Michigan's Thumb.* N.P., [1969].

Soini, Paul, ed. *Bad Axe Golden Jubilee.* Bad Axe, 1935.

How Carp Came to The State

Annual Report of the State Board of Agriculture of Michigan. Lansing, 1884 & 1891.

Cornfeld, Lilian. *Israeli Cookery.* Westport, Conn. 1962.

Drews, Robin & Petersen, Eugene. "The Carp in Michigan," *Michigan History Magazine*. Vol. XLI. No. 1 (Spring 1957). p. 91.

Hubbs, Carl L. & Lagler, Karl F. *Fishes of the Great Lakes Region*. Ann Arbor, [1958].

Michigan Biographies. 2 Vols. Lansing, 1924.

von dern Borne, Max. "Raise Carp!" *United States Commission of Fish & Fisheries. Report of the Commissioner for 1880*. Washington, 1883. p. 673.

Father Francis O'Brien, Renaissance Man

Barbara, Sister Mary. *A Covenant With Stones*. Nazareth, 1939.

Celestine, Sister M. "Rt. Rev. Monsignor Frank A. O'Brien, M.A. LL.D," *Michigan History Magazine*. Vol. VI. No. 4, (1922). p. 611.

Grapevine. Commemorative Issue. July 1989.

Massie, Larry B. & Schmitt, Peter J. *Kalamazoo: The Place Behind the Products*. [Woodland Hills, CA. 1981].

May, Katherine, compiler. *Historical Data Concerning Borgess Hospital. 1889-1977*. Unpublished typescript.

Pare', George. *The Catholic Church in Detroit 1701-1888*. Detroit, 1951.

Quinn, B.I. *Substitution For Marriage*. Kalamazoo, 1881.

Swantek, Wanda. *The Sisters of St. Joseph of Nazareth 1889-1929. A Chronicle*. Nazareth, 1983.

Joseph Bert Smiley: Poet With A Punch

"Bert Smiley Takes His Life." *Kalamazoo Gazette*. 9 May 1903.

Hodgman, Francis. *To the Citizens of Galesburg & Vicinity*. (Broadside). [Lansing, 1893].

Jones, David. L. *Rip-Roaring Rhymer: The Story of Joseph Bert Smiley*. Unpublished manuscript draft, 1991.

"Joseph Bert Smiley," *Kalamazoo Daily Telegraph*. 3 August 1895.

Massie, Larry B. & Schmitt, Peter J. *Kalamazoo: The Place Behind the Products*. [Woodland Hills, CA. 1981].

Portrait & Biographical Record of Kalamazoo , Allegan & Van Buren Counties... Chicago, 1892.

[Rogers, Isaac B.] *The Solemn Truth*. Vol. 1, No. 1 & 2. 7 January & 19 January 1895.

Smiley, J.B. *A Basket of Chips...* Kalamazoo, 1888.

_____. *Meditations of Samwell Wilkins*. Kalamazoo, 1886.

_____. *Nora...* Galesburg, 1895.

The Great English Sparrow Hunt

Barrows, Walter B. *Michigan Bird Life*. East Lansing, 1912.

Brewer, Richard, McPeek, Gail & Adams, Raymond. *The Atlas of Breeding Birds of Michigan*. East Lansing, 1991.

Bull, John & Farrand, John. *The Audubon Society Field Guide to North*

American Birds. [N.Y., 1977].

Cook, A.J. *Birds of Michgan*. Michigan Agricultural College Experiment Station. Bulletin 94. April 1893.

Cook, C.B. "The English or House Sparrow," *Twenty-Ninth Annual Report of the State Board of Agriculture*. Lansing, 1890.p. 275.

Cumming, John. *This Place Mount Pleasant*. Mount Pleasant, 1989.

Dearborn, Ned. *The English Sparrow As A Pest*. USDA Farmers' Bulletin 493. Washington, 1915.

Granlund, James, McPeek, Gail & Adams, Raymond J. *The Birds of Michigan*. Bloomington, IN., [1994].

Judd, Sylvester D. *The Relation of Sparrows to Agriculture*. USDA Biological Survey. Bulletin No. 15. Washington, 1901.

Kuhn, Madison. *Michigan State: The First Hundred Years*. East Lansing, [1955].

Laycock, George. *The Alien Animals*. N.Y., [1966].

Massie, Larry B. & Schmitt, Peter J. *Kalamazoo: The Place Behind the Products*. [Woodland Hills, CA., 1981].

Michigan Legislative Manual... Lansing, 1897.

"A Plea For the Birds-English Sparrows," *Fifth Annual Report of the Pomological Society*. Lansing, 1876. p. 457.

Schmitt, Peter J. *Back to Nature: The Arcadian Myth in Urban America*. New York, 1969.

Wood, Norman. *The Birds of Michigan*. Museum of Zoology, University of Michigan, Miscellaneous Publication No. 5. Ann Arbor, 1951.

When Fresh Water Sailors Battled on the High Seas

Feuer, A.B. "Our Only Option Was To Attack," *Michigan History*. Vol. 80. No. 5 (Sept/Oct 1996). p. 8.

Freidel, Frank. *The Splendid Little War*. Boston, [1958].

Michigan Biographies. 2 Vols. Lansing, 1924.

Millis, Walter. *The Martial Spirit*. Boston, 1931.

Official Souvenir Michigan Volunteers of '98. Detroit, [1898].

Stringham, Joseph S. *The Story of the U.S.S. Yosemite*. Detroit, 1929.

Utley, Henry M. & Cutcheon, Byron. *Michigan As A Province, Territory & State...* 4 Vols. N.P., 1906.

Trowbridge: The Dam Story

Bush, George. *Future Builders: The Story of Michigan's Consumers Power Company*. New York, [1973].

Deming, Brian. *Jackson An Illustrated History*. [Woodland Hills, CA., 1984].

Greater Kalamazoo. Supplement Kalamazoo Daily Gazette. 30 July 1904.

Hager, David C. *Next Stop Kalamazoo: A History of Railroading in Kalamazoo County*. [Kalamazoo, 1976].

Luther, E. Hardy. "Early Developments in High Voltage Transmission," *Michigan History*. Vol. 51, No. 2. (Summer 1967). p. 93.

When Vincent Price Said Tryabita

Andreas, A.T. *History of Chicago*... 3 Vols. Chicago, 1886.

Dr. Price's Delicious Desserts Containing Practical Recipes... Chicago, 1904.

Illinois vs. Michigan Indoor Dual Meet (program). Ann Arbor, 1903.

Leonard, John W., ed. *The Book of Chicagoans*. Chicago, 1905.

Massie, Larry B. & Schmitt, Peter J. *Battle Creek: The Place Behind the Products*. [Woodland Hills, CA., 1984].

_____. *Kalamazoo: The Place Behind the Products*. [Woodland Hills, CA., 1981].

Price, Vincent C. *The Paradise of Health*. N.P. [1910].

Swope, James. *Yorkville, Michigan: The Age of the Mills*. (unpublished paper).

Horseless Humor & Car-Toons

Caricature: Wit & Humor of a Nation in Picture, Song & Story. Annual Vols. New York, [1906-1915].

Donovan, Frank. *Wheels For A Nation*. N.P. [1965].

Marquis, Albert Nelson, ed. *Who's Who in America*. Vol. VI, 1910-1911. Chicago, [1910].

Nevins, Allan. *Ford: The Times, the Man, the Company*. New York, 1954.

Olson, Sidney. *Young Henry Ford. A Picture History of the First Forty Years*. Detroit, 1963.

Partridge, Bellamy. *Fill'er Up!* NewYork, [1952].

Pulitzer, Walter. *My Auto Book*. New York, 1908.

Rae, John B. *The American Automobile: A Brief History*. Chicago, [1965].

Stoddard, William Leavitt, ed. *The Motorists' Almanac for 1917*. Boston, 1916.

Sullivan, Mark. *Our Times: Vol. 4. The War Begins 1909-1914*. New York, 1932.

Welsh, Charles. *Chauffeur Chaff or Automobilia*. Boston, [1905].

White, J.J. *Funabout Fords*. Chicago, 1915.

The Dowagiac Bishops & the *Titantic* Tragedy

Draeger, Carey L. "They Never Forgot: Michigan Surviviors of the Titantic," *Michigan History*. Vol. 81. No. 2. (March/April 1997). p. 29.

Everett. Marshall, ed. *Wreck & Sinking of the Titantic*.N.P. [1912].

Hamper, Stan. *"The Sinking of the Titantic & the Dowagiac Connection"* (unpublished article).

Kishpaugh, Richard. Interview. Allegan Forest. 1 Feb. 1998.

Lord, Walter. *A Night To Remember*. New York, [1955].

Lynch, Don. "The Tragic Marriage of Helen & Dick Bishop," *Titanic Commentator.*

Marshall Logan. *Sinking of the Titantic...* N.P., [1912].

Wade, Wyn Craig. "The Senator & The Shipwreck," *Michigan History.* Vol. 63. No. 6 (Nov/Dec. 1979). p. 11.

The "Bare Torso King" in Battle Creek

Carson, Gerald. *Cornflake Crusade.* New York, [1957].

Deutsch, Ronald M. *The Nuts Among the Berries.* New York, [1967].

Lowe, Berenice Bryant. *Tales of Battle Creek.*[Battle Creek, 1976].

Macfadden, Bernarr. *Vitality Suprem.* New York, [1915].

Macfadden, Mary & Gauvreau, Emile. *Dumbbells & Carrot Strips.* New York, [1953].

Massie, Larry B. & Schmitt, Peter J. *Battle Creek: The Place Behnid the Products.* [Woodland Hills, CA., 1984].

Stoltz, Garth. "A Taste of Cereal," *Heritage Battle Creek.* Vol. 2. Spring 1992. p. 46.

Wilkinson, Joseph F. "Look At Me," *Smithsonian.* Vol. 28. No. 9. Dec. 1997. p. 136

When A President's Morals Went On Trial

Ashlee, Laura R., ed. *Traveling Through Time. A Guide to Michigan's Historical Markers.* Lansing, [1991].

Holli, Melvin G. & Tompkins, C. David. "Roosevelt vs. Newett: The Politics of Libel," *Michigan History* Vol. 47. No. 4. (December 1963). p. 338.

Lewis, William Draper. *The Life of Theodore Roosevelt.* Philadelphia, [1919].

Marquette *Mining Journal.* 25 May - 3 June 1913.

Morison, Elting E. *The Letters of Theodore Roosevelt.* Vol. VII. Cambridge, 1954. p. 671.

Pringle, Henry F. *Theodore Roosevelt A Biography.* New York, [1931].

Rydholm, C. Fred. *Superior Heartland A Backwoods History.* 2 Vols. Marquette, 1989.

Thayer, William Roscoe. *Theodore Roosevelt An Intimate Biography.* Boston, [1919].

"There Is No Such Thing As A Bad Boy"

Cramer, Luella M. "The Starr Commonwealth," *Holland's Magazine.* January, 1924.

Fennimore, Keith J. *Faith Made Visible: The History of Floyd Starr & His School.* Albion. [1988].

Hollinshead, Ann. "Floyd Starr, '10, Social Scientist, Friend of Boys." *Io Truimphe* (Albion College Alumni Magazine). July, 1938.

McAdam, Elizabeth & Starr, Floyd. *"...No Such Thing."* Cleveland, 1968.

Starr News. Vol. 36. No. 4 (December, 1980).

Starr, Floyd. *"Memories"* Unpublished typescript. Undated.

Starr Commonwealth News. Supplement. Vol. 3. No. 11   (Spring, 1947).

Stogie Stories

Heimann, Robert K. *Tobacco & Americans.* New York, [1960].

Huckett, H.C. *Further Studies Concerning the Aphiscidal Properties of Tobacco Dust.* New York State Agricultural Experiment Station, Geneva, N.Y. Technical Bulletin No. 121. August, 1926.

Massie, Larry B. *Haven, Harbor & Heritage : The Holland, Michigan, Story.* Allegan, 1996.

Massie, Larry B. & Schmitt, Peter J. *Kalamazoo: The Place Behnd the Products.* [Woodland Hills, CA., 1981].

Report of the Michigan State Commission of Inquiry into Wages & the Conditions of Labor for Women... Lansing, 1915.

Salesmen's Educational Manual. M.A. Gunst & Co. N.P., 1917.

State of Michigan *Annual Report of the Bureau of Labor & Industrial Statistics...* Lansing, 1896, 1905, 1908, 1909, 1915.

When Billy Sunday Slid Into Detroit

Billy Sunday's Sermons As Reported by the Detroit Times... [1916].

Ellis, William T. *"Billy" Sunday: The Man & His Message.* N.P. [1914].

Englemann, Larry D. "Billy Sunday: God, You've Got A   Job On Your Hands in Detroit," *Michigan History.* Vol. LV. No. 1 (Spring, 1973). p. 1.

Persons, Frederick T. "Sunday, William Ashley," *Dictionary of American Biography.* Supplement 1. p. 679.

Rodeheaver, Homer. *Twenty Years With Billy Sunday.* Winona Lake, Ind., [1936].

Father Patrick Dunigan: Fighting Chaplain

Gansser, Emil B. *History of the 126th Infantry in the War With Germany.* Grand Rapids, [1920].

Hagerman, Donald, R. Interview. Kalamazoo. 12 January 1995.

[Hanton, Carl]. *The 32nd Division in the World War. 1917-1919.* [Milwaukee, 1920].

Honor Roll of Kalamazoo County. 1917, 1918, 1919. N.P., [1920].

Landrum, Charles H., compiler. *Michigan in the World War.* N.P., [1924].

Obrecht, Frances H. *"Padre."* Philadelphia, [1935].

Tentler, Leslie W. *Season of Grace: A History of the Catholic Archdiocese of Detroit.* Detroit, [1990].

Influenza Pandemic of 1918

Burr, C.B. ed. *Medical History of Michigan*. 2 Vols. Minneapolis, 1930.

[Clark, Faye] *As You Were: Fort Custer*. Galesburg, 1985.

Honor Roll of Kalamazoo County. 1917, 1918, 1919. N.P,, [1920].

Ninety-Five Years of Nursing Education 1890-1985. The Butterworth Hospital School of Nursing. [Wyoming, MI. 1986].

"The Plague of Influenza," *The American Review of Reviews*. November, 1918. p. 467.

Sullivan, Mark. *Our Times... Vol. V. Over Here 1914-1918*. New York, 1933.

Swantek, Wanda. *The Sisters of St. Joseph of Nazareth 1889-1929: A Chronicle*. Nazareth, MI. 1983.

Woodward, Frank B. & Mason, Philip P. *Harper of Detroit*. Detroit, 1964.

Teenie Weenies In the North Country

Cahn, Joseph M. *The Teenie Weenies Book: The Life & Art of William Donahey*. LaJolla, CA., 1986.

Carter, James L. *Voyageurs' Harbor: A History of the Grand Marais Country*. Marquette, 1977.

Donahey, William. *Teenie Weenie Town*. New York,   [1942].

_____. *The Teenie Weenies*. Chicago, 1917.

Erikson, Fern. "Barrel Built For Two Curio In Grand Marais," *Grand Marais Pilot & Pictured Rocks Review*. 7 Oct. 1994. p. 3.

Everyman's House

Balls, Ethel & Lassfolk, Marie. *Living In Kalamazoo*. [Kalamazoo, 1958].

Crane, Caroline Bartlett. *Everyman's House*. N.Y., 1925.

Massie, Larry B. & Schmitt, Peter. *Kalamazoo: The Place Behind the Products*. [Woodland Hills, CA. 1981].

Rickard, O'Ryan. *A Just Verdict: The Life of Caroline Bartlett Crane*. Kalamazoo, 1994.

Schmitt, Peter J. *Kalamazoo: Nineteenth Century Homes in a Midwestern Village*. [Kalamazoo, 1976].

The Football Game That Should Never Have Been Played

Behee, John. *Fielding Yost's Legacy to the University of Michigan*. Ann Arbor, [1971].

_____. *Hail To The Victors*. Ann Arbor, 1974.

Dodd, Robert Lee & Wilkinson, Jack. *Dodd's Luck*. [Savanah, GA.,1987].

Donnelly, Walter A. *The University of Michigan An Encylopedic Survey*.   Vol. IV. Ann Arbor, 1958.

Kishpaugh, Richard. Interview. Allegan Forest. 1 Feb. 1998.

Peckham, Howard. *The Making of the University of Michigan*. Ann Arbor, [1967].

INDEX

278

Born in Grand Rapids, Larry B. Massie grew up in Allegan. Following a tour in Viet Nam as a U.S. Army paratrooper, he worked as a telephone lineman, construction laborer, bartender and in a pickle factory before earning three degrees in history from Western Michigan University. In 1983 he launched a career as a independent historian, specializing in the heritage of the state he loves. He lives with wife and workmate Priscilla and their 35,000 volume library in a rambling old schoolhouse nestled in the Allegan State Forest. Sons Adam, Wallie, Larry Jr. and daughter Maureen insure there is never a dull moment.

Larry B. Massie enjoys "spreading the Gospel of Michigan history" via storytelling.

Larry B. Massie's
MICHIGAN HISTORY BOOKS AVAILABLE FROM THE PRISCILLA PRESS

White Pine Whispers 288 pages, ill. bib. index. $12.50
Hardbound Limited Edition $18.95

On the Road to Michigan's Past 288 pages, ill. bib. index. $12.50
Hardbound Limited Edition $18.95

Birchbark Belles 310 pages, ill. bib. index. $12.50

Potawatomi Tears & Petticoat Pioneers 296 pages, ill. bib. index. $12.50

The Romance of Michigan's Past 270 pages, ill. bib. index. $12.50

Pig Boats & River Hogs 296 pages, ill. bib. index. $12.50

Copper Trails & Iron Rails 290 pages, ill. bib. index. $12.50
Hardbound Limited Edition $18.95

Voyages into Michigan's Past 298 pages, ill. bib. index. $12.50

Walnut Pickles & Watermelon Cake: A Century of Michigan Cooking 354 pages, ill. bib. index, $19.95

Warm Friends & Wooden Shoes: An Illustrated History of Holland, Michigan 128 pages, 8 1/2 x 11, ill. bib. index, hardbound. $18.95

Shipping on individual books $2.00
Two or more books ordered retail - shipping is free
Michigan residents please add 6% sales tax

Order from Priscilla Massie
2109 41st Street
Allegan Forest, Michigan 49010
(616) 673-3633
Please indicate if you would like the author to inscribe the books.